Create Your Happiest Life from the Inside Out

LIVE FROM YOUR HEART AND LOVE YOUR LIFE!

LYNDA FORD

BALBOA
PRESS

A DIVISION OF HAY HOUSE

Copyright © 2018 Lynda Ford.

All rights reserved. No part of this book may be used or reproduced by any means, graphic, electronic, or mechanical, including photocopying, recording, taping or by any information storage retrieval system without the written permission of the author except in the case of brief quotations embodied in critical articles and reviews.

Balboa Press books may be ordered through booksellers or by contacting:

Balboa Press
A Division of Hay House
1663 Liberty Drive
Bloomington, IN 47403
www.balboapress.com.au
1 (877) 407-4847

Because of the dynamic nature of the Internet, any web addresses or links contained in this book may have changed since publication and may no longer be valid. The views expressed in this work are solely those of the author and do not necessarily reflect the views of the publisher, and the publisher hereby disclaims any responsibility for them.

The author of this book does not dispense medical advice or prescribe the use of any technique as a form of treatment for physical, emotional, or medical problems without the advice of a physician, either directly or indirectly. The intent of the author is only to offer information of a general nature to help you in your quest for emotional and spiritual well-being. In the event you use any of the information in this book for yourself, which is your constitutional right, the author and the publisher assume no responsibility for your actions.

Any people depicted in stock imagery provided by Thinkstock are models, and such images are being used for illustrative purposes only. Certain stock imagery © Thinkstock.

Print information available on the last page.

ISBN: 978-1-5043-1228-8 (sc)
ISBN: 978-1-5043-1227-1 (e)

Balboa Press rev. date: 03/08/2018

This book is dedicated to:

Mum and Dad - both so generous with love, support and wisdom throughout the years. Mum's encouragement of a path less travelled; Dad's consistent rational enquiry; both taught me the value of integrating the heart and mind so one can be proud to live life authentically.

Jonah and Teangi - my beautiful children; my friends; my enduring inspiration.

And to those I have loved and lost who have coloured my world with happiness, challenge, change and insight..

To all of these I am forever grateful.

Contents

Introduction

"To live is the rarest thing in the world.
Most people exist, that's all."
– Oscar Wilde.

You are standing right now at a pivotal crossroads. Do you settle for a mediocre life, just existing and tolerating circumstance that cause you unhappiness? Or will you decide instead, to crank up the volume on a meaningful life of your own making? To really *live* is a choice. You can continue on the same road you always have, it will be predictable and familiar, but nothing will ever change for the better. To be happy and live well, it helps to discover the 'why' behind all you do and take responsibility for where you are right now. After all, *existence* is a mediocre substitute to *thriving*!

It is commonly drummed into us throughout childhood to fear making mistakes. This can result in excessive caution in taking *any* risk at all. When such caution limits our pursuit of meaningful activities that can provide us with fulfilment, challenge and growth, we end up missing out on many wonderful opportunities to feel really alive! I won't be suggesting jumping out of a plane just to face our fears (but of course you can if this is something you've always wanted to do!) Rather, this book is about something far more enduring that can lift us from the depths of despondency and help discover the source of any discontent we may feel. Even when we feel life is pretty good, we sometimes still wonder why it is we lack excitement about our future. Many people have come to accept that the only 'high' one feels is when they artificially induce it, but this is only the case when we live an *ordinary* existence. We can become wired instead, to *expect the extraordinary!*

My hope in this book is to reconnect you to who you are at your core. This will stimulate a renewed awareness of what motivates you and how putting yourself first will ensure you have the maximum energy, love and respect for all the people and activities you engage with. Motivation grows naturally when we connect with meaningful objectives, but most of us no longer really know what *gives* our life meaning. Re-acquainting with such self-awareness will leave a lasting legacy on our attitude, the decisions we make in the present and the actions we choose to take in the future.

Happiness is directly anchored to personal freedom. Such freedom comes when we begin to live more consciously and give ourselves permission to explore our hopes, desires and dreams. When did you last ask yourself questions that were reflective and meaningful? Here's a few to consider:

- ❖ What would I love to do more of?
- ❖ What would I have to change to ensure I can?
- ❖ Which parts of my everyday existence do I dislike?
- ❖ Is there any part of my life that feels like a square peg in a round hole?
- ❖ Does my day go too fast or do I look forward to it being over?

Honest self-reflection is the first and hardest hurdle to scale. Perhaps you don't yet know what would make you happier, but you know what is causing you stress and discontent. That is a good start!

As a positive self-empowerment advocate and life-long student of holistic wellbeing, I have grown increasingly familiar with some of the reasons why people are not living a life they love. This book provides key insights into the most productive principles behind empowered living. It explores how to find the courage to change those areas you should, as well as practical self-care and awareness strategies that will support your journey on a passionate, self-directed future.

To create an extraordinary existence, there is one key ingredient for success: to engage your heart with your mind. Your heart sees the world a lot differently to your mind. It will entertain ideas even when they appear impossible at first glance. Whereas the mind is driven more by logic, reason, security, significance and certainty. All of these have a respected role to play in influencing decisions, but they shouldn't be allowed to dominate at the expense of stifling your heartfelt inspiration.

> *"If you limit your choices only to what seems possible or reasonable, you disconnect yourself from what you truly want and all that is left is a compromise."*
> **– Robert Fritz.**

When you develop trust in your heart driven inner voice, feelings of self-assurance naturally follow, lessening the dependency on certainty in order to feel happy. The mind has a tendency to be drawn towards familiar experiences, as habitual participation in such activities is more likely to provide you with feelings of comfort and certainty, but the latter is merely an illusion born from repetition. Certainty really never exists, any more than the likelihood that humanity will agree to follow the same form of religion. Consider how many marriages have dissolved due to complacent attitudes which grow from feeling too familiar and secure. People often remain in a job because it is 'what they know'. They might tell you it is for security of income, but it is more likely the subconscious addiction to familiarity. There is nothing wrong with this, so long as they genuinely feel happy with where they are injecting daily energy and making each moment count. The intention is for us to become conscious directors of experience, as opposed to allowing choices to be driven simply by a need for certainty. One is dynamic and responsive, whereas the other is dependent and fearful.

How happy we feel depends largely on how we spend our days, as this governs how productive and purposeful we feel. For some, the 'daily grind' is something to be endured, hitting the pause button on 'real life' when at work. The trouble is, feeling this way will cause tension to build within us like steam does in a boiling kettle and pressure must be released in some physical way. No-one wants life just to pass them by. Our heart will always fight to be heard above the noise of a busy existence that lacks meaning. Grumbling about the way things are may help us to feel better in the short term, but words of complaint will not change the circumstance, only inspired action will. Being in a state of stress can disable our ability to overcome problems. So we will explore why stress impairs our judgement, keeping us stuck in circumstances we don't like and how we can overcome its stronghold.

Developing an ability to self-reflect, cultivate optimism and take inspired action when we are most in need of positive change, will ensure we do not become doomed to frustration and disillusionment. It is clear that the happiest people are those who don't necessarily have all the 'bells and whistles', but who experience contentment from the security of knowing who they are and what motivates them to action. Self-awareness is a precious gift, but we must reach within our own heart to find it. Each one of us deserves to explore our hopes, dreams and gifts, but we will never manifest them while we remain blind to what they are. Come to understand them as a purposeful driving force and not only will we experience a heartfelt connection to our life that we never have experienced before, but best of all, we will become the most authentic version of the person we were destined to be.

To those of you saying right now that 'my responsibilities come first, I would be selfish to put myself before them', I'll say this: there is a distinct point of difference between being self-aware and selfish. You can be considerate of others' needs, whilst also learning more about what you need to give the world the *best of you*. I invite you to become engaged as the new CEO of your life, rather than just letting the tide take you were it will. It will take courage and passion on your part, two things never found inside your head, only within your heart. Dreams and inspiration spark only within the heart. True understanding and compassion can only be found by connecting with your heart. Excitement, bliss and intention, grow only by energising heartfelt emotions. The power of life is expressed by the physical pounding of the heart- it makes you feel alive! What so of the mind? It is a filter through which you sift thoughts and emotions. It can transform or restrain you, often falling into a reactive pattern based on past experience. The more you become conscious of the thoughts you keep, steadily your mind becomes trained to serve you more positively. Whereas your heart is pure, simply needing you to attune to *its frequency*. It is not that these two are enemies but rather you need them working effectively together to reinstate balance. The secret lies in allowing your heart to guide your mind, rather than letting one's mind be the dominant force of logic, as it will drown out the voice of the heart.

Live first from your heart, see choice as your guiding light and let change be your friend. When thoughts are driven by your heart and not constantly filtered or even blocked logically by your head, they can become inspired, compassionate, intuitive and clear. I hope that this book will engage your heart every step of the way. Life is to be loved, not just tolerated. Let's make this journey really matter!

Part 1

AWAKENING

∞ Our Happiness Begins with a Choice ∞

Life is but two sides of a coin. We simply respond or react dependent on how we view the call of the toss. Neither side is bad or good until we have interpreted it to be so by our choice.

Life means to make no argument with the side that lands, for it knows either side will bring what we need right now for our greatest growth. But we command the choice, if we shall indeed grow or diminish by the experience that comes our way.

For what is the purpose of this existence, if not as a learning curve to expand who we are? We can trust that change is natural, or feel victimised by our trials and tribulations. It is our choice to be self-directors, or otherwise outsource our governance to others who will gladly take us to where *they* wish to go.

Our heart holds the wisdom of an ageless soul and yet our mind fights hard to deny the existence of spirit in this physical plane. External conflicts are a given while we have the greatest conflict still going on inside of us – denial of our true self.

The nature of our world is such, that without belief in some greater meaning and without faith, we become lost. Meaning gives us reason and motivation to act, whilst faith gives us the persistence to see our intentions into fruition.

Our capacity to see good coming from even the worst
of experiences, can ignite within us a deep inner power
despite our circumstance. Insight will then follow,
attuning us to *who* we are and *why* we are here.
This insight is pure, purposeful and positive. It can
raise us above the restraints of reactivity and enable us
to deal only in the currency of responsiveness.

Such response is cultured to help us stay centred and calm no
matter the storm. From this quiet centre we retain our composure,
consciously making decisions, seeing new opportunities as they
arise. We become surrounded by options, not dead ends.

A heart-driven life will never fail to grow in such fertile
ground. Optimistic response is to see adventure, not adversity;
feel compassion in place of judgement; choose freedom over
fear; and have faith that every mistake is but an important,
profound step of progress on our beautiful journey.

Trust in your heart's guidance and make your choices.
Dare to fall down and courageously get up again.
There my friend lays your road to true happiness.

Chapter 1

HAPPINESS ALWAYS EXISTS, BUT IS ELUSIVE TO FIND.

"The more you make happiness a target, the
more your aim is likely to miss."
– Viktor Frankl.

We do not really need to go searching to find happiness. It has a way of finding us even when we least expect it. Targeting happiness often occurs when we look outside ourself for external things to stimulate happy emotions and this habit can become addictive. What we all really want is the power to feel happy even in the midst of imperfect conditions. Happiness can mean different things to different people and what triggers happiness for one person will not for another. The reason for this is that our enduring happiness is closely aligned with personal fulfilment. Such fulfilment is nourished by our own unique values and spiritual beliefs. But if we instead seek fulfilment in transient elements, such as material wealth, the more precarious will be our moments of happy feelings. Once we can attach happiness to the things we have full control over, such as our own thoughts, attitude and the meaning we give to life, the more enduring will be our experience of happiness.

Abraham Maslow was an American psychologist who developed the five level theory of a hierarchy of human needs. For us to self-actualise and be happy (fifth level), he believes we have to first fulfil the previous four levels of basic needs. This first level begins with meeting base physical needs like food, water and shelter and then progresses to the second level of creating a safe and secure environment. The third level follows as we develop friendships and a sense of belonging. The fourth level is the creation of positive self esteem from feeling valued and experiencing success. Maslow says that only when all of these needs are met, will we be able to reach our greatest potential of morality, wisdom and show compassion towards others. In essence, he is inferring that there are many external conditions which are important to be in place if we are to be happy and be in a headspace to contribute to the betterment of ourselves and our fellow man. Maslow's theory is but one piece in the happiness puzzle. Sure it makes sense that feeling safe, healthy, loved and wealthy, all add to our happiness, but we know that all of these things can be with us one minute and gone the next.

An unexpected turn of events can create a sequence of unfortunate losses. Consider this: we have been working for a company for ten years when it goes into receivership and we lose our job. We can't find other work. Our partner only works part-time, so our financial debts become more than we can afford. This results in defaulting on our mortgage repayments. The emotional turmoil and financial insecurity leads to many arguments in the household and a marriage breakdown ensues. Stress causes our health to take a nosedive. This situation is a huge challenge, but it does not have to result in such a cascade of negative outcomes. Maslow's type of happiness is built upon the strength of maintaining our 'needs' fortress, but once it comes unstuck, we find ourselves unprepared to cope. The best way to build our resilience to the possibility of loss is to strengthen those internal attitudes that will help us to endure our ups and downs. Throughout history, we have heard brave tales of people who have managed to rise above terrible life conditions, such as homelessness, poverty, slavery and violence and not only persist, but also develop the tenacity to break free of such limiting circumstances, inspiring others to reach for their dreams as well.

In Howard Cutler's book *The Art of Happiness*, he interviews and documents the Dalai Lama's perspective and insights on this topic:

"Achieving genuine happiness may require bringing about a transformation in your outlook, your way of thinking and this is not a simple matter. You need a variety of approaches and methods to deal with complex negative mental states. Change takes time."

In essence, the Dalai Lama believes that lasting happiness comes from patient, persistent mental discipline, approaching attitudinal change day by day, moment by moment, learning as we go to deal with our reactions to life conditions. Certainly our attitude governs much of the way we respond or react to what is going on around us. Once we make a commitment to reigning in reckless negative thoughts, this activates our ability to stay more positively in control of daily triggers that would normally upset us.

Mahatma Gandhi, on the other hand, likes to view happiness from this perspective:

"Happiness is when what you think, what you say and what you do, are in harmony".

He believes happiness comes from being authentic, or true to ourselves. Indeed authenticity is at the heart of our own happiness, as it ensures we act in alignment with our values and positive beliefs. Our thoughts, our words and our actions should reflect such ethics. They should not be piecemeal whereby we say the right words but act in a completely different way. As a parent I have always considered it important to behave in the same way I expect my children to behave, otherwise it's just lip service in asking them to do what I am not prepared to do. Children do not respect parents who have one set of rules and values for their kids and then a different set for themselves.

The easiest way to recognise if you are living authentically is to observe your thoughts, words and actions. Are they in harmony with each other and with your core values? I will share an idea of what I mean. Perhaps one of your core values is 'love your work' and yet you stay in a job you hate and speak as though it is impossible for you to change it. You tell your kids how important it is that they find a rewarding career and assure them they can do anything they set their mind upon. However, when your kids do tell you what career they would love to pursue, you disapprove, trying to steer them down a more traditional path.

We often have an idealistic, value-driven vision, but somehow we stop it becoming our reality due to a lack of belief in ourselves or others to achieve it. This causes frustration to build up. We know that we are compromising. That is why self-reflection helps us to live more authentically, because it reminds us to be honest with ourselves. Every person has a unique way of looking at the world. Authenticity respects who we are and calls upon us to love that person, rather than hide him or her away just so we can become more like everyone else. Only once we become conscious of who we are can we become the best version of ourselves, by noticing what needs to change for the better.

Martin Luther King Jr famously said:

> **"Our Lives begin to end the day we become
> silent about things that matter."**

Silence in this context can be interpreted as complacency, lack of compassion or belief that we cannot make a difference. The things 'that matter' however, are not just *world ethical issues*. We can relate this sentiment much closer to home, such as speaking up for our *own* needs in life, or to the challenge of *communication with those we love* to understand and solve problems. When we withdraw from an opportunity to effect a change, or communicate in a considered manner, over time we develop feelings of regret, resentment and even guilt. In our hearts we know we are choosing the easy path that demands less of us and pretends we don't care. It is the road of denial and it is a lonely one to tread. Not only do we become more self-serving but we remain stunted, retreating from opportunity and contribution, rather than taking inspired action to make our lives and world a better place.

We all seek greater meaning behind our earthly existence even if we are not yet conscious of it. Finding meaning to fuel our thoughts transforms them into inspired action the fastest of all, as it is the highest motivational force and the quickest path to discovering happiness and fulfilment. In the Western world, we suffer from one major ailment. We are mostly lucky to have enough to *live by*, but are sometimes lacking true meaning in our life to *live for*. Personal meaning differs for every individual. For some, finding meaning relates to pursuing a spiritual path. For others, connecting with their own unique passion to drive their daily activities is the ultimate. Some people are happy simply making the most of whatever daily tasks they are involved with, so long as they give it their best and feel they are contributing positively to their community, family or friends. Really, it is possible to read greater meaning into anything we do, if we just take more notice of the little things that provide us with opportunities to be more appreciative. For instance, not many of us enjoy housework, but even the most menial tasks can be transformed into rewarding, enjoyable and tolerable activities if we learn to feel gratitude for both the end result (having a lovely fresh, clean house) and the privilege of having a roof over our head. Gratitude is a close sister to meaning, reminding us that nothing should be taken for granted and this practice can be used powerfully to inject our world with more happy emotions.

So it appears that happiness does not have to be so elusive after all, but our ability to *feel* happy is enhanced by what we choose to focus on at any given moment. Living more consciously, aware of the thoughts we think and the values we hold dear to our hearts,

Chapter 2

BECOMING MORE CONSCIOUS OF WHY WE DO WHAT WE DO.

Open eyes and an open heart brings clarity to our life that clears the path for the journey ahead.

Why do we allow ourselves to accept mediocrity, when we have the potential to love what we are doing from day to day and create extra-ordinary experiences? We cleverly slide into a zone which we will call *pretend detachment.* It is a state of mind that enables us to disconnect from the pressure and pain that comes when we give up expecting the best. I say *pretend,* because all of us know the truth inside our heart but may choose to ignore it. From this place of detachment, we give ourselves a warped sense of not being in control of our life. We then become increasingly excuse driven and less aware of the real reasons behind our actions or inaction.

The first major step in activating a happiness state that endures is to be honest with ourselves. This leads to conscious self-appraisal, enabling us to take action in areas of our life that need change. What follows is a collection of behavioural traits. A primary connection maybe felt with just one of them or in a lesser degree to a few. They are not shared to make anyone feel bad, on the contrary, they are intended to assist give us insight into areas that might kick-start some honest self-reflection. Our more negative behaviours are often triggered by false assumptions and the only way we moderate or get rid of them is by understanding *why* we tend to do the things we do!

First we have the BUSY person.

Most of us are busy, right? But should we allow ourselves to be so caught up in it that we don't slow down for long enough to discover we may not be happy? Being busy feeds our sense of feeling significant, productive, important and irreplaceable. All of these can provide us with feelings of satisfaction, but the very nature of being excessively busy is that we become stressed and lose touch with who we are and what we want. We can easily fool ourselves into thinking being busy means being fulfilled because when we are not busy, we deactivate due to feeling exhausted.

Then we have the patient WAITER.

Some of us spend our lives waiting. Waiting for circumstances to improve of their own accord. Waiting for external factors to change and become perfect, offering us more time, less responsibilities, more money, no mortgage or an empty nest. Only then will we give ourselves permission to do what we really want to do. This habit simply puts goals on hold. It ensures that less than ideal circumstance is tolerated and activities that would be more meaningful to us are postponed. Other people and current circumstance are allowed to dictate when we have the go ahead on growth and change. It's considered that we are hostage to life and simply have to bide our time.

Others like to play VICTIM to circumstance and BLAME.

It is easier to blame something or someone else for our predicament. The 'If only I had had a better childhood, better self esteem, was succeed at something new can further escalate, when we judge our ability based on our previous failures.

The good news is that none of the above behavioural tendencies define us as who we are forever, they just allow us the insight to understand what beliefs are casting an influence upon us at the moment. No-one forces us to run ourselves into the ground at a flat out pace. We make the choice to deny our greater hopes and aspirations for a better life, tolerating mediocrity instead. Procrastination is really built upon excuses and to continually wait until conditions are perfect just seems like an easier option. *Pretend detachment* tricks us into feeling everything is OK, when really we are allowing ourselves to dismiss what positive change we need to make our life intentionally more colourful.

There are five very important attributes that we can work at cultivating that will help us to give our *pretend detachment* the flick for good. They will generally only awaken within someone who has made a *conscious decision* they are worthy to live a rewarding, extraordinary existence. These five attributes will be noted as you progress through sections of this book and in most instances several chapters will be devoted to the strengthening of that one particular attribute within you. These special five are: **Volition, Attitude, Vitality, Vision and Inspiration**....or VAVVI for short! The first of these you may have noticed at the beginning of this chapter was *Volition* and by its very meaning requires us to step up and use the power of our own will to make *conscious decisions* that take full responsibility for the changes we need.

> **When we couple conscious living with tuning into our heart, we create a strong, unshakeable will which motivates us to take action on that which matters to us the most.**

To live consciously means to be aware and informed. It is that state where we no longer make excuses for our situations and recognise that things happen as a result of our thought focus, which influences where and when we take action. Conscious living is the awareness that this moment responds to us, equally as much as we respond to it. It constantly provides us with feedback to tell us what is working and what isn't. Ultimately, it is up to us to decide if a situation demands further persistence to get the most from it, or whether we need to change direction completely. Our circumstances are but a flow of events which collectively build character and insight, offering new opportunities every step of the way. The trick is to keep moving forward and don't let ourselves get stuck in regret of a decision made, instead, *simply choose to make a new one.*

Attuning to our heart helps us to do this more easily than if we depend on our logic. Call it our gut instinct. It is real and it knows what you need. It is far more subtle but persistently hovers in the back of your mind, questioning the adamant direction of your logic. It yearns for one thing...for you to find meaning in your life. So when you align conscious living with heartfelt insight, you unleash a powerful intent to make decisions based on meaningful outcomes.

Chapter 3

GIVE YOURSELF PERMISSION TO SEARCH FOR MEANING.

Once we accept that life is meant to be a journey
of discovery to find true meaning, we awaken to
our birthright to experience true happiness.

Meaning makes life worth living as it puts the pep in our step and injects our days with enthusiasm and joy. Do you remember at school when you were forced to study subjects and concepts which you could not relate to, or understand where, when or how you would ever use that knowledge? It was boring and seemed a total waste of time because it was not relevant to your direction or interests. I know I reached that point at school where I simply had that feeling I was just treading water and being forced to put off the discovery of something far more important- the meaning of MY LIFE! Sure there is a great deal of solid foundational knowledge we all need to learn at school to give us a good start, but there is a reason why some kids excel at Maths, Science, others at English, some at Art, Drama or Woodwork. We are all unique and are born with different natural abilities. As children mature and try to figure out their career direction we could be asking questions that liberate a plethora of possibility: 'What interests you and excites you the most? What do you think is your greatest talent you could share with the world? Is there a problem that you would love to help solve?' We all have special gifts and it is up to each individual to give themselves permission to discover and take ownership of those wonderful gifts. As parents, encouraging our children to develop the courage it takes to step into their full power and discover their natural abilities and passions, is *our* greatest gift we can give to them. The best way to do this is by example. Walk the talk! If we put our own dreams on hold until our children are all grown up, we will do nothing but show life is a compromise.

Howard Thurman said it so well:

> **"Don't ask yourself what the world needs, ask yourself what makes you come alive and then go and do that, because what the world needs is people who are alive."**

A lot of time and attention seems to get invested in convincing young adults to follow a certain career path, simply for reason of income security and certainty of direction. In the process of pleasing others, many of us lose heart, forgetting what ideas inspired us the most when we first launched into this big world. We start out believing the 'world is our oyster' only to spend our time doing things which seem pointless, stressful, distracting and de-energising. Even worse, we often prioritise these activities over tasks that otherwise would bring us joy and contentment. Instead of expanding into our true potential as a person, we shrink and diminish, reducing our ability to stimulate the best in ourselves as well as the best in others. Our lives must have personal meaning and purpose if we are to feel fulfilled and happy.

Viktor E. Frankl was a Professor of Neurology and Psychiatry at the University of Vienna Medical School. He also spent three years during World War II in concentration camps, including Theresienstadt, Auschwitz, and Dachau, where believe it or not, he formulated many of his key ideas in his approach to help liberate people from their own self-imposed suffering. Logotherapy, as it became known, is founded on the belief that our main motivation for living *is our will to find meaning in this life*. To endure this horrific experience in the Nazi concentration camps, he had to pool every last inner resource he could muster. He discovered that it is what we tell ourselves about the present moment and our belief in not only a future, but a purposeful reason for persisting, that is all that stands between life and death when we teeter on the cusp of despair.

For some of us, it is enough to consider our spark of existence is sacred, thus would never conceive of giving up. For others, it is people or things that we are greatly attached to. In yet other instances, we may feel we have unfinished business to take care of and that prevents us from taking our leave early. Generally, the more we have that we believe is worth fighting for and worth hanging around to enjoy, the less likely we are to consider suicidal thoughts. But in the case of Viktor, in the hellhole he found himself trapped in, what did he still have to live for? In his well known book "Man's Search for Meaning" it tells of his predicament: *His father, mother, brother, and his wife all died from malnutrition or had been sent to the gas ovens, so that, apart from his sister, his entire family perished in these camps. How could he- every possession lost, every value destroyed, suffering from hunger, cold and brutality, hourly expecting extermination- how could he find life worth preserving?'* He began to think more in terms of protecting the last vestige of his beliefs, which were the one thing they could not take from him and the only thing left that he could still control. He remembers a pivotal moment when he said to himself, *'No matter what you do to me, you cannot make me live in hatred!'*

Viktor began to understand that we are more than a reactive being and no-one else can find life meaning for us, as this we must connect to ourselves, much like plugging a lamp into an electric power point to shine forth the light. Without the electrical current which can be considered as 'meaning', we do not discover our true potential, our existence lacks purpose and we are more inclined to give up.

"There are only two ways to live- one as though nothing is a miracle, the other as if everything is."
– Albert Einstein.

If we place life on a pedestal classifying it as being the true miracle that it is, then feelings of unhappiness should be the exception, not the rule, for complacency should not grow when we respect and cherish something. Unhappy feelings generally come from focusing on what we don't have, so the key is to fill any void with the knowing that we are rich beyond measure in being alive every day! Have you ever asked someone 'How's things?' and they have surprisingly responded with 'I'm great! I woke up this morning so couldn't be happier!' We don't often hear that do we, but we *should.* Life is amazing and miraculous and we owe it to the forces of creation to explore it with child like abandon and excitement, expressing daily gratitude for our opportunity to be here on Earth and accepting our responsibility to make our existence really matter.

I lost my mother to breast cancer ten years ago. She was taken too early from this world at age sixty nine, less than a month before she was due to have her seventieth birthday. If you'd known my mum, you would know her as someone who lived fully and embraced life energetically. She had been very fit and active, absolutely loved gardening and had a natural green thumb. She was also a very loving, caring parent whom I had many long discussions into the night with, in wonderment of what life was really all about when I was a just a teenager. I remember our attempts at meditating together, we would put a tape cassette on to listen to Ian Gawler for guided meditation (an amazing man who had experienced cancer and survived) and in the process of quietening our minds, we would find it hard not to burst out laughing during the beginning of the meditation. Even if one of us could contain our mirth, the other would lose it instead, setting off the other. The words and voice that Ian used would just stir us up when he said "just let yourself relax deeeeeply and compleeeeetly, letting yourself gooooooo." We were like two naughty little school girls trying to muffle our giggles so the teacher did not hear. In the end we realised the only way we were going to have a productive meditation was to do it in separate rooms!

Mum wasted no time procrastinating about chores and projects that needed to be done, she just got on and did them. I do not believe she had many regrets when it came to the end of her days, only that she had not finished living yet! She had been diagnosed with primary breast cancer in her forties when I was just thirteen years of age. This first time around she managed to kick cancer's butt via recommended orthodox treatments: chemotherapy, radiation and a partial mastectomy, but she also adopted natural dietary changes as well to help support her immune system. I am sure this assisted her greatly, but twenty years on the cancer returned and this time it proved too persistent.

From this experience of losing my mum and a great friend, I began to realise how you cannot afford to take anything for granted. If you are not exploring what makes your world sparkle, then you are missing the point. Why put off your 'real living plans' until retirement either, that is a cop out. Not only that, but just remember that you may never see your retirement years. You have to make life matter in the here and now, not later.

Both Science and Religion has drawn on their own methodologies of research, belief and historical data to explain how our miracle of existence has occurred, but nonetheless, they are still equally fascinated by it and neither can define or understand everything there is to know about Life. Religion largely uses faith to fill in the gaps, whereas Science continues researching in hope that *one day* they will discover every last secret behind Creation. Perhaps that is the way Creation works though, she will never reveal all her secrets to those living, that way we will maintain eternal awe for the gift we've been given!

Do you consider this life to be a miracle or do you feel detached from wondering about why we are here? Many people might say, 'I haven't time to consider such things, I am too busy and have more tangible, physical needs to focus on anyway.' But what if it actually did make a difference? Is it possible that giving thought to this one belief above all other thoughts that race through our heads, may indeed be the very miracle you have been waiting for, to bring more happiness into your world?

I am not of any religious denomination, but nor am I a person who needs scientific fact to explain every last detail of our physicality. I am curious and believe there are remarkable and amazing forces at work to create our Universe and to animate every living being here on Earth. Life slips past so quickly, that I believe Love is the only thing that is real and the only thing which makes life matter. I speak here of Love for oneself, for other people, for all other living creatures and the miracle of life on this beautiful planet.

My personal belief is that we are spiritual beings having a human existence and somehow we commonly share a tiny drop of this miraculous 'self-aware' force of animating energy. This common thread of connection between every individual has the power to unite humanity despite of our differences, because it tells us that there must be a bigger intention at work to express creatively and with love and meaning. In other words, there must be a greater purpose behind everything we do. As such, if we start living with our eyes wide open, we begin to take notice of synchronicities and new opportunities to grow, reflect and learn from events that occur. I much prefer this belief than the alternative of considering everything is just random chance or planned acts of fate that we have no control over.

Even if you don't believe we are spiritual beings (and I have no wish to impose my beliefs upon you) I am suggesting that our existence is beyond our comprehension to fully explain. Therefore, it demands to be revered and made the very best of whilst we are given the opportunity to explore it. Further to this, if you do not believe in reincarnation, then wouldn't you be even more driven to make

or *safe* problems, the main difference is that a *safe* problem involves self-imposed suffering brought on by not taking action to rectify the issue. We play a victim to our circumstance, keep getting upset with the situation, but meanwhile tell ourselves we are powerless to change anything. Such excuses can only be faced with honest self-reflection. Examples of safe problems are when we experience depression, engage in addictive behaviour, blame our issue on someone else, avoid decisions, pretend we are happy when we are not and withdraw from relationships.

Quality problems on the other hand are a different kettle of fish. A decision regarding a *quality* problem would create forward momentum, something which will bring change and positive transformation. They literally take our life to a new level and will challenge us to confront internal fears. These problems will only be overcome when we open our mind to new perspectives and information which provides the insight needed to solve them. Connecting to our own heart driven values is an important part of this process. Such decisions may relate to the following: career changes; relationship challenge; making a commitment to life goals, beliefs and habits which align with the most positive version of us; choosing a completely new direction from the past; and forgiveness, of ourselves and others.

The first step to transform a *safe* problem into a *quality* problem is to recognise which of these two it is. Is it keeping us stuck in repeat mode, feeling a victim; or is it a challenge because it is more of a 'process' issue brought on by being in unfamiliar territory where growth could occur? The wonderful thing about the two types of problems is that they are more closely aligned than we think. Really, the major key difference between them is a willingness to do what it takes to create a solution that we can take action on, then any problem we have transforms into a *quality* one. To be really committed to change, there are a few steps we need to take.

❖ Firstly, recognise that there *actually exists a problem and we choose to take responsibility for it.* As was noted earlier, this may seem elementary, but denial or lack of interest to really know what the problem is, means we will not get rid of it anytime soon. It means we either don't yet know how to fix it or we fear the change that will be required from the outcome to solve it.

❖ Secondly, *be willing to develop a strong 'why' the problem needs to be fixed.* If we don't know why we should bother fixing it, we won't. Same goes for making a change at the request of another person wanting us to change... it will not last unless their *why* becomes our own genuine motivation because it made logical and heartfelt sense to us.

❖ Thirdly, we *must believe it is possible to overcome the problem.* Without a positive mindset that believes it is only a matter of time before we will discover the right solution, we will be doomed to fail.

❖ Lastly, *there exists a willingness to brainstorm creative solutions and take action!* If we lack genuine belief in any of these steps, we will fail in fixing our issue. Problem solving really does start with us taking *ownership* of the situation. We gain nothing from playing blame games. Of course this doesn't mean we will not have challenges along the way, but it does require that we create the right frame of mind to ensure we remain *committed* to find a conclusive solution.

When the issue involves another person, it is about approaching the conversation in a collaborative, open minded way, rather than going in with 'all guns a blazin' to make them feel bad. It is not about who is right or who is wrong, but more about growth and awareness to better illustrate a 'win win' benefit to both of you moving forward. You cannot control the way someone chooses to respond to you, nor can you make them change their behaviour, but you can control the way you relate and respond to them. Sometimes we need the courage to admit that change *within us* maybe necessary too. In the end, we feel much better about ourselves if we have taken action and extended the hand of unity by trying to problem solve an issue that is affecting more than just ourselves. When such positive change is resisted, the best solution could be to remove ourselves from a negative situation. Interestingly, the more pro-actively we approach problem solving with an attitude embracing growth, the easier we will accept the outcome, even if it is not the solution we originally were hoping for.

Brendon Burchard, in his book 'The Motivation Manifesto', encourages us to overcome the fear of challenge and elevate our capacity to endure:

"And so we want freedom from pain and yet will celebrate meaningful struggle and hardship because we know those very things will free us from one level of life and set us into another."

Struggle is positive when we are liberating ourselves from something which is holding us back. Whether this be your own negative mind talk, external circumstance or relationships. We are unable to experience heartfelt living, if we are not prepared to shed the very things which are contributing to feelings of limitation and unhappiness.

Journaling can be powerful medicine.

When we clarify and admit to having some difficult problems, our intention should be to get them out of our head and down onto some paper. I like to call this our 'Express Journal'. Well after all, is it not better to outpour to a journal first to vent strong emotions, rather than dump such intense, raw feelings on someone we respect who has offered to lend a friendly ear? A Journal is a valuable self-help method to expose an issue to ourselves. Write comprehensively and it will read back as a story and snapshot about this moment in time. The distance it can provide us when we read it back in a more level-headed state the next day is invaluable. It tends to make us feel like we are listening to a friend's problem as they vent to us. Feeling more detached from the issue without the intense emotion puts us in a much more effective state to brainstorm ideas and solutions. Keep in mind, that negative stress is actually a gift. When we learn to isolate the issues which currently cause us the greatest stress, we can then choose to either *erase* such stress or *manage* it better by focusing our initial efforts and energy to problem solve.

Sometimes our problems can appear exceptionally complex and we may have spent considerable time trying to solve them to no avail. This is when I would recommend talking about them with a third party, such as a life coach or counsellor, as it can be very beneficial to gain a new perspective from someone completely outside your familiar circle. If you presently do not feel ready to do this, try consciously to put your problems aside for a little while. You should take a break from trying to work through them and skip ahead to Part 2 of this book. There you will find ideas to take time out to increase your vitality. Chronic stress can be damaging so it is more immediately important to manage the tension it causes by learning ways to help relax your mind and body.

Many people suffer from the delusion that when they find themselves in a life position they don't like, that they are suddenly a captive victim to it and that becomes the problem more than the problem! Stress feasts on such feelings and affects both your mental resilience and your physical stamina, eroding your capacity to be creative and solution oriented. The lesson to be learned is that stress is not to be ignored- it is a sign that something needs to change. The more negative stress we endure, the deeper we embed ourselves into a self-made pot hole. Volition is what saves us from sinking deeper into it. Kick your will into gear and transform your stressful issues into life change you know you need.

Chapter 5

TAKE RESPONSIBILITY FOR LIFE CHANGE YOU NEED.

"Change will not come if we wait for some other person or some other time. We are the ones we've been waiting for. We are the change that we seek."
– Barack Obama.

When we are born, we are granted a powerful ability to hold influence over our life direction, by making conscious choices that lead to life changes we need. Along the way though, it can be easy to lose touch with our ability to make such choices. This can be due either to lack of personal willpower; lack of belief that we actually have the option of choosing change; or by allowing others' opinions to have sway over our decisions. It is quite common that we will decide *to do* or *not do something* based on what we think is for the common good, rather than what is right for us. If we allow someone else to make our choices, then it is much easier to blame them if things go pear shape - which of course can be quite appealing! However, when we choose to take full responsibility for our choices, it means we live with the awareness that we *have* created and everyday *are creating,* our present and future experience.

What if our spiritual beliefs don't always support this notion? It is possible that they may work against us at times and allow us the fuel to blame our negative life predicaments on more noble factors. For instance, if we believe in *fate,* or *karma* - both of these can become great scapegoats for why stuff happens *to* us. Blaming a karmic debt is an easy way to move into victim mode, as we may think our situation is something that must be endured. Same for believing that our fate is set in stone...this doesn't serve us well as we forego any control of our situation. The term 'God's will' can underpin both beneficial beliefs and negative ones. On the upside, it can provide us with patience to tolerate less than desirable circumstance that (for now) may appear outside our control, but the down side is we may feel that we *should not even try* to alleviate the pain, as it is something that God wishes us to endure.

If we believe we cannot do anything to improve our situation, we gradually become very resentful, no matter our personal beliefs about Creation. *A slight shift in perspective can enable us to harness a belief to serve us better.* Imagine that life is made co-creatively. It is possible that some of our problems may evolve from deeper karmic connections, or even God's intentions for us to experience certain challenges, but let's try to see them more as lessons, not barriers. The more problems we are exposed to, the greater our progress can be, as challenges can be the most effective catalyst for growth and insight to understand ourselves and others better.

> *Choice is the outcome of free will and fate is the outcome of choice. We are the designers of our own fate whilst our Creator merely observes. Do not blame others- your life is your own.*

I wrote this when I was in my early twenties and have lived by this philosophy, feeling totally accountable for everything and every feeling I have ever experienced. I also know that not every experience is meant to be a 'breeze'. If we do consider that life is meant to be a school of learning, then we can start approaching our problems with curiosity and look for the lessons to be learnt from and within our experiences. For that is the only way we grow as human beings - feeling pushed to understand our situation, which then in turn fuels an inner yearning to improve, rather than blindly accept it. This is the only way that change ever occurs. It begins with the awareness of a discontent deep inside of us and a strong sense that we are no longer happy with the way things are. This is a message from your heart telling you *not* to settle. To succeed at creating lasting positive change, you must become aware of a motivation behind your discontent- the 'why' is extremely important to provide both persistence and resilience needed to see you through the change required. We will explore this in greater depth in Chapter 7 because it is *your why* which enables you to continue towards your goal when challenged or fearful.

There are those occasions when no matter what we do, we cannot change the outcome. We simply have to accept it and move on as best we can. An example of this is when we lose a loved one. We can feel as though we will never be happy ever again. This is very normal emotion and we cannot expect to move through grief quickly. But knowing that we are not alone in having to endure grief and loss, does help us to overcome the intensity of our feelings over time.

> *Where there is life, there must also be death, just as the sun rises, so does it set. Grief is real, but as each day passes let your pain transform, to know that our loved ones don't die, they simply change form.*

I felt ripped off when my mum was taken early from this life because of breast cancer. It did impact my feelings for a time, it felt unfair, it felt completely final and unchangeable. While she was battling cancer I had at least felt I could choose to take positive actions of influence to increase the odds of her surviving. But once her body eventually succumbed to the cancer, I then felt guilty that I had failed her somehow, that I should have tried harder and done something different to help her to heal and live. Inside my heart I really knew I had done all in my power to help liberate her from the condition she was battling. The one thing I know from my personal experience of grief is that if we are given the opportunity (like I was) to make every moment matter with a loved one when their prognosis has not been positive, then seize that chance. Make every moment count and talk about all the things that are important, both to you and them, no matter how trivial. For even when one believes in life after death as I do, their death still feels terribly final during our own lifetime.

We all have our 'demons' to overcome. Challenges come upon us whether we like it or not and we do not always have a choice in the matter. Grief is but one example. A sad fact though is that not all change seems fair, it may leave us feeling powerless, victimised, sad and angry. But we still control how long those negative feelings last for and how we choose to re-direct that emotional energy, to avoid letting circumstance start dictating a negative slide in our outlook. The key is to not let these experiences rob our own life of positivity forever. Some experiences have to be endured and negative emotions freely expressed if we are to then heal and discover our positive, happy self again. *The more we learn to express how we feel, the quicker healing takes place.* Negative emotions which are ignored get sent underground, embedding into our subconscious. They are then prone to influencing our thoughts in ways which express resentment and disillusionment, contributing to further depressed states.

Becoming conscious of chronic negative emotions, means we must first *acknowledge having them.* There is nothing shameful to see them and realise that they may have been our way of coping with a bad situation. However, only we can choose to break such a cycle by recognising our ability to rise *up and out* of our negative state and resume optimism again. We cannot change everything, nor stop bad things from happening to us, but we can control how we think about them and to what degree we allow them to affect us negatively. The following Serenity Prayer sums up the first expectation we should have of ourselves:

> *"God grant me the serenity to accept the things I*
> *cannot change, the courage to change the things I*
> *can and the wisdom to know the difference."*
> **– Reinhold Niebuhr.**

There are those events which we have very little, or no control over. If we do not learn to accept them, we remain in a very unhappy state for a long time. We cannot prevent our loved ones from dying when their time has come, any more than we can avoid a collision caused by another driver running a red light. We might complain loudly when we're given the news of our retrenchment, but we can't do much about the situation if our employer is financially ruined. Neither can we always avoid relationship breakdown... we can't force someone we love to change, or equally expect our partner to love us when they no longer do. Acceptance is one of the hardest attributes to cultivate and one of the most important. It should not be confused with *blind* acceptance though, which is when we presume we are powerless to effect a change in a positive way, simply because we feel pessimistic about our ability to make a difference to an outcome. This is where a little wisdom is needed!

Let's use relationship breakdown as an example from above to explore what I like to call the state of *courageous acceptance*.

What if our partner told us they would like a divorce? First we feel surprised, then confused and finally rather shattered. We don't understand what went wrong and did not think things were *that* bad, but our partner tells us they have had enough and can't live with us anymore. We say that things can be different, we will change, let's give it another chance... but our other half is definite in saying we had plenty of opportunities to turn things around but we didn't. Then comes the kicker... they have fallen out of love with us anyway, that's it.

So this sounds pretty definite doesn't it? Certainly, there may not be much hope that the relationship will ever heal, let alone re-unite and our partner does not give us any signs that this could be the case. We still are given a choice though. We can carry through our bitterness and resentment into the future believing we were mistreated unfairly, acting awkward and unpleasant whenever we pick up or drop off the children. We can refuse to increase our understanding of why the relationship took a turn for the worse, by acting in the very ways which are negatively expected of us. This will ensure we approach any new relationship in an old school way, blocking new insights and dooming us to repeating the same behaviours that contributed to the demise of our marriage in the first place. Now in this context, if we were still really hurting underneath our angry exterior and secretly wished our partner would fall back in love with us... I would have to say that is not likely to happen. While we choose to stay exactly the same, we are sabotaging any chance for a reunion to ever occur.

Now on the other hand, there was another path we could have chosen. After taking some time to get over the hurt, we could have developed interest into what makes relationships tick. Rather than thinking we were right and our partner was wrong, our open mindedness could result in new insight and different behaviour. This doesn't mean we shoulder all the blame, but rather we actively seek to understand what factors contributed to our partnership demise, even if just to make sure we don't repeat this with someone else. Meanwhile we express greater tolerance and extend friendship towards our ex- partner, learning to forgive and also trying to cultivate the compassion to see the breakdown through their eyes as well as our own. The separation does not have as negative effect on the kids, because 'mum and dad' can talk and be friendly.

This is one way we can show 'the courage to change the things you can', as we have complete control over our own behaviour. We certainly have the power to make choices that result in less negative impact upon others, without compromising our own self respect. By doing this, change and growth occurs, breaking any negative

∞V.A.V.V.I.∞

ATTITUDE:

"A Settled way of thinking or feeling about something- a perspective, belief, point of view, mood or pose."

∞V.A.V.V.I.∞

Chapter 6

CHOOSE A POSITIVE, PRO-ACTIVE PERSPECTIVE.

*It is not what you get dealt in life but
how you choose to deal with it.*

Our attitude underpins the meaning we attach to all our experiences. Do we see the beautiful rose in bloom, or the angry thorns? Do we curse the bee that stings us on the foot, or do we rejoice they are active in our garden pollinating the fruit trees and vegies? Attitude is a pattern by which we think about and develop a perspective upon every single area of life. It leads us to interpret and view what happens to us through our own unique filter that is created and influenced over the course of our lives. Ingrained beliefs build from our attitudes, to provide us with something solid to refer to, every time we have need of a response to whatever is going on around us. They become an easy quick reference guide to judge what happens to us, as good, bad or indifferent and how best to deal with it. If we change our basic attitude, we can change our beliefs and paradigms much easier, to ones that serve us rather than block us from seeing the joy that exists.

As we discussed in the previous chapter, to be able to overcome our problems we must first recognise and take responsibility for them. But what benefit will this bring to us if we still have a negative, victimised attitude? We will not have the inner fortitude to see beyond the immediate problem, or develop the self-reflective capacity to brainstorm solutions. Attitude is really one of two things, being either positive or negative. Our attitude helps us to interpret what meaning we choose to place upon events and experiences, so we can create presumptions about them. This governs if we respond thoughtfully or react emotionally. Our attitude manages our behaviour post-experience as well, underpinning the type of thoughts we have, words we use and actions we take. Our enduring beliefs then build from such events and the results we get, which then ensures we get more of the same attitude we started with and the cycle begins to maintain support for either mostly negative or mostly positive perspectives. It's not un-alike a lawyer building their case in the court of law, except *your subconscious mind* is the lawyer and it assembles evidence mostly on autopilot!

The circumstances and changes that we are confronted by are all neutral experiences. It is our interpretation of them that makes them good or bad. Once we can accept this truth, we can also take responsibility for the way they make us feel, the meaning we apply to them and what we choose to do in response to them. Attitude underpins all our presumptions of what can or can't happen. It dictates when we will choose to take action to help fix a situation, or when we will dismiss an idea even before we give it due consideration.

Here is a life scenario, where I will point out how easy it can be to get caught up in negative presumption: *You are working full time and feel that you do not have enough time to spend with your family or time for yourself. Your job is quite stressful and busy. By the time you get home you're exhausted and cannot keep up effectively with household chores, let alone do other activities which are important to you. You are not eating as healthily as you should and this is compounding your lack of energy along with working too hard.*

We can fall into the trap of presuming any suggested solution will never work. Dismissing ideas can cause us to wallow even more in worry, as it makes us feel we are less able to fix anything and remain stuck in our depressing predicament. Our spouse makes a suggestion - instead of working full time, request a cut back of hours to permanent part-time and have one day off a week. 'No way' you say. 'I can't afford to lose a day's wage! Management would never agree to that anyway.' How do you know they would not agree to the change in work hours unless you actually ask? *This is a negative presumption and so is the thought that it is impossible to exist on less income.* Another suggestion then gets put forward - every member of the family could pitch in more to help with housework, gardening, cooking or any other chores necessary so we all share chores equally. When we hear that comment the first thing that pops into our head is 'Hell is likely to freeze over first!' With that type of attitude we will doom it to fail for sure. *We have negatively presumed again that it is impossible,* thus, we are unlikely to ever try starting a family discussion on the issue. Unfortunately, by presuming the worst we have also robbed our family of a real opportunity to show more generosity with their time and show that they do care. Unfortunately, from one negative presumption, more negativity tends to grow.

Some people may disagree with me, but I think we *can* change our attitude, from being mostly negative to mostly positive, simply by making the choice to do so. Of course it is natural sometimes to feel peeved, down, or frustrated. But once we are more conscious of such feelings, we can choose to reduce how much time we allow ourselves to stay with those thoughts. By redirecting our attention to seek the up-side to a situation, we develop a pro-active perspective revealing new options and possibilities. This new positivity will help recalibrate our mind so it sits more firmly in the creative zone of resolution.

I understand that some people are diagnosed with psychological depression which can make it especially challenging to maintain mental balance and optimism. In such cases, medication can sometimes be the first and best option. It may assist to bring equilibrium back into one's emotions and state of mind in the short term, but long term it is important to consider other holistic methods that can complement medication or assist support our intention to having made a mistake which effects us; or perhaps our child might think twice before they disclose honestly to mum/dad again after we completely lost your cool with them! Keep in mind, that although we may interpret a situation as us being wronged, it is possible *we* maybe wrong about that. It is always harder to take back what has been said and done after the fact. Isn't it better if we learn to respond to that which goes on around us, so we don't get so much negative fallout and experience rollercoaster emotions?

In the case of dealing with circumstances we are unable to change, all we can really do is rely on our positive attitude and the meaning we decide to give it, to enable us to tolerate a less than ideal situation. Viktor Frankl offers this insight:

> *"Everything can be taken from a man but one thing- the last of the human freedoms- to choose one's attitude in any given set of circumstances. Everybody in the midst of suffering is given a chance to bear testimony of the human potential at its best, which is to turn a personal tragedy into a human triumph. When we are no longer able to change a situation, we are challenged to change ourselves."*

He believes suffering is a natural part of our journey, but it is up to us as individuals to find meaning in the suffering that we endure. To elevate beyond our suffering, it helps us to consider how we can make something much better out of the unpleasantness we have endured, so it is not experienced in vain. This helps in such times that we find ourselves at our lowest point, losing all motivation and feeling at a loss to expect anything more from our existence. It is during such an experience that it is worth considering that life may still want something *from you*. Our highest motivational force is to contribute in some way and make our days matter. So perhaps the key is to transpose our own personal tragedy into a guiding light for others to follow.

We can hit our PAUSE Button.

I heard this technique first explained by Mary Morrissey, who has been in the personal development and self-empowerment industry for over forty years as a Teacher, Inspirational Speaker and Author. We have an in built capacity to press a pause button on our emotional reactions. So when we are told news that appears only negative; or something happens that changes the course of our day and future plans... we can choose to hit "PAUSE!" The idea is to put off our explosive upset for three days and if we still feel as frustrated and negative about the situation, we then have permission to express our emotions to our heart's content, so long as it harms none! The intent of this technique is to block our negativity about the situation for three days and focus on allowing the possibility that something good could come from the change of circumstance into our psyche *first*, before our negative mindset gets in the way.

A useful, short and sweet affirmation to repeat over to ourselves in reminder here could be:

∞ *I am sure there is something good that will come from this* ∞

This is the quickest way to reign in negative thoughts and actions which could further jeopardise an already tenuous situation. Why let one unfortunate event upset our whole day, week or year? Unfortunately there are times when we cannot afford to hit our pause button for three days. We need to reflect on what may have just happened and make a decision quickly. To do this and be happy with our decision, we still must place a pause on our negativity so that we do not jump to hasty conclusions. The objective is to *slow down our emotional reaction*. All such reactions are generally fuelled by immediate fear of change which can make us tip either towards sadness, anger or panic. We are physically affected with increased tension in muscles and generally feel us feel more positively productive. There are suggestions made in Part 2 of this book that can assist us to feel more physically energised and relaxed. This can lead to being more naturally productive in using what time we have more effectively. Perhaps this will lead to feeling so vital that less sleep will be required! (This is not a joke.)

Overcoming our greatest block to productivity is procrastination... sometimes we spend so much time thinking about doing things that we never actually move onto the 'taking action' phase. A vicious circle begins to emerge when we have so many things on our to-do list that we get confused about which task to start on first. Most times it feels easier to avoid those chores/tasks we least enjoy and they start to mount up. In Chapter 13 we explore why it is so important to 'clear the deck' on a regular basis. This will enable us to remain focused and on track in the key areas that matter.

As we cultivate positive mastery over how we spend our time, it will become necessary for some to examine their inability to say 'no' to external demands on their time beyond the daily routine of family needs and work. This can be especially important for those who have either a big social circle, extended family, or a lot of community commitments. Becoming selective in how to spend the spare time we do have is essential if we are trying to create more opportunities for positive change. Nothing degrades a positive attitude quicker than when we feel powerless over the size of our miniscule 'time share' and are spread too thin over too many duties!

Many people who knock positive thinkers, do so because they call them out as unrealistic dreamers. But really, all a 'dreamer' is, is someone who *desires to live a life of meaning and has an attitude which positively reflects that expectation.* So when we consider that in regard to all we have been discussing, who wants to be limited in their vision by a negative disposition? Can it really do any harm if we let ourselves dream big dreams, see expansive possibilities which are not limited by current circumstance...even if only 10% of that which we intended, ever came to pass? Is that not better than a big zilch, zero, nada, nothing, as would be realised if we had no vision whatsoever? That is the reality for a negative thinker. They see all the bad things first and imagine the worst case scenario which stops any thoughts of possibility in their tracks. The beauty of being a dreamer is that the only thing which separates us from dream transformation, is action! They are not so very far apart.

Chapter 7

EMBRACE CHALLENGE AND FEAR.

*"Our greatness lays not so much in being able to remake
the world... as in being able to remake ourselves."*
– Mahatma Gandhi.

The Story of Fire.

The Banksia is an Australian Native plant which can be found growing in the most inhospitable terrain. Existing in salt laden coastal landscapes, to harsh and hot inland deserts, in all shapes and sizes- from majestic trees, right down to soil-hugging, hardy ground covers. They have the most interesting, bird attracting, bottle-brush like flowers that come in many different colours. If this contrast of adaptability to challenging conditions, tempered with the rugged beauty and uniqueness of its blooms was not enough, it also has another very clever trick up its sleeve...it requires fire to regenerate. Yes, woody Banksia seed cones need to experience the heat of fire to release their seed, after which they will find growth easier as they proceed to fall into and take root in the high potash-rich soil that only exists after a bushfire has ripped through the landscape. Not exactly a smooth ride to establish themselves!

So it is often with us...we do not always experience smooth sailing, but everything that transpires does have its purpose and every challenge we live through and overcome, affects who we are and how we relate to our world. Are you allowing your challenges to expand and grow who you are, or have you succumbed to letting such experiences burn you, build resentment, or overwhelm you with fear at the thought of the risks that come with them? Challenge and change can be our best friends, but only if we are able to see them for what they truly are... opportunity. They are not sent to purposely overwhelm us. Every opportunity comes both with a choice and equal potential for positive or negative outcomes.

Fear and risk will always exist.

If we choose to anchor our mindset in the fear and risk of failure before we take action towards the change we need, guess what? This will ensure we never take any action at all, or if we do, we doom ourselves to fail based on negative expectation injected in every thought! Remember the Banksia, it has turned a harsh reality into an opportunity to transform itself and regenerate. Time and natural evolution has assisted its potential to do this of course, but nonetheless, it has now mastered the challenge that confronted its very ability to persist, harnessing bushfire to strengthen its vitality rather than diminish it.

The story of the Banksia helps to illustrate the fact, that fear and risk are certainties that accompany our existence, whether we like it or not. We cannot expect all that we do to be easy, nor should we hope for it to be, for there is a lot to be gained from our challenges. Fear is also a very natural emotion. As a human being, we would not live very long in this world if we did not acknowledge feelings that warned us of physical danger and sometimes it is our 'gut instinct' which also warns us of an especially risky situation which could affect us physically and/or mentally. Familiarity, however, can reduce our perception of fear greatly, to the extent that certain activities no longer *seem* like a risk to us anymore. We could call this a false sense of security, as in most cases the risks do not disappear; we just become complacent to them. For instance, think of driving a car.

of it every day. (The fridge or back of the toilet door works really well!)

In fact four things will increase the power of any commitment:

1) Writing down the intention or goal.
2) Knowing why it is so important to make a change.
3) Aligning your 'why' with your heart driven values.
4) Deciding when you will begin and what action will be your first to take.

Our greatest fear should be the possibility that we do *nothing* and *never* take a voluntary risk, because with no challenge, we do not grow. Instead we remain safe and the same forevermore. Our self confidence only remains whilst we are doing something familiar and as soon as we step outside of that 'bubble', we can't cope. So rather than allow our confidence to grow 'organically' from new experience, it stagnates and becomes stunted, which creates more fearful attitudes if things don't remain the same. That is why some people find it almost impossible to cope when a sudden change occurs in their world which was not of their own making, such as loss of their job, or a breakdown in their relationship.

> *"It must be born in mind that the tragedy of life doesn't lie in not reaching your goal. The tragedy lies in having no goals to reach. It isn't a calamity to die with dreams unfulfilled, but it is a calamity to not dream. It is not a disgrace not to reach the stars, but it is a disgrace to have no stars to reach for. Not failure, but low aim is sin."*
> **– Helmut Schmidt.**

Just like maintaining physical fitness, it has been said time and time again, 'use it or lose it!' You could say the same goes for our *change muscles*. The less we use them, the weaker they become and the harder we find it to be adaptive to new circumstance. The more we stride forth purposefully to achieve the positive changes we aspire, the better we cope with all types of change, even that which we don't choose. To feel a little fearful and to be aware of risk involved with a decision is natural. True happiness will only be found by testing our boundaries, so that we can hope to expand beyond them. Sometimes we really *do* need to feel the fear and do it anyway!

Chapter 8

CONTROL YOUR THOUGHTS.

"Every morning is a new beginning, a new chance for you to re-write the story of your life".
– Tina Su.

It helps to remind ourselves regularly, that the past does not dictate our future, nor does the circumstances surrounding us right now. Our present situation has been influenced by the mental focus we have held up until this very day, driving our thoughts into actions. From this day forward, however, we can create a new future experience, dependent upon *defining and aligning with who we wish to become*, not who we have been.

Anything which has occurred in our past has now gone for good and can no longer be changed. But the memories held about it can provide invaluable lessons to ensure we don't repeat the same mistakes. They underline the importance of transforming what we go through into something better and more positive. I like this insightful quote by Deepak Chopra:

"I use memories, but I will not allow memories to use me."

There is much wisdom and power behind these words. We all have memories, some good and some not so good. However the question we should be asking ourselves is which ones are having the greatest influence over our daily thoughts? Are we using memories of past experiences to positively influence future action, or are they slowing us down instead and casting doubt and negativity on our present day progress? Some people spend more time watching reruns in their minds eye, than they do focusing on the present moment and planning their next positive step forward.

There tends to be three levels of interaction with our memories:

1st Stage: Feeling the raw emotion that we felt during the experience like it was happening now, or still reacting with emotional judgement of actions taken. We may still harbour feelings of regret, guilt, blame and have difficulty reconciling issues.

2nd Stage: Remembering and reminiscing often, still attuned to the emotions we felt during and surrounding the experience, but with increasing detachment and less intensity.

3rd Stage: Remembering and reminiscing once in a while, with less emotional expression and mostly in a thoughtful and reflective way.

As time passes we normally move through these three stages of healing and come to a point that we resonate more with the last stage, enabling us to remember past experiences, but without all the negative baggage that goes with it. If it is our *own* past actions and behaviour that we are not so proud of, at least we can choose to learn from what happened and gradually use such knowledge to avoid making the same mistakes in our future. The power of insight and reflection is a force to be reckoned with, but the stagnation and negativity that comes from wallowing in regret, will grind us to a halt. This then prevents us from acting in new ways, so that we remain on replay mode *all the time.*

So what do we do if we realise we are stuck on replay… retreating to memories and bashing ourselves up over past actions, decisions, lost opportunities and never really solving recurrent issues? Acknowledging that we are doing this is a fantastic start. Owning the raw emotions that we still have and why they might still be alternatives on paper can really create a lot more clarity in moving forward and be able to let go of un-important thoughts. Our worry journal can provide a powerful method to deal with thoughts which are constantly interrupting our day, but help divert them to be considered at a better time in the day on our terms. This means we no longer need to be entertained by re-runs fighting for our attention all day long.

Feeling Gratitude.

Sometimes our worries are just not worthy of our attention at all.

> *"Worry is like a rocking chair: it gives you something to do, but it doesn't get you anywhere."*
> **– Evan Esar.**

When we are being trivial stress-mongers, *that* is the right time to change our focus. Another way to do this is by making a habit of searching for all the good things we are grateful for in our lives. Gratitude is wisdom which will always overpower negativity. Consider breaking our *worry journal* into two sections- one half for our worries and the other half for feelings of gratitude. At the end of each day, we simply write down what we feel grateful for. Start with five things and then build up to as many as we can think of. If we make the effort to take this journal with us wherever we go, it means we can then break our patterns of rehashing old memories and feeling negative from unsolved problems, by reading and focusing instead about what we do feel happy and grateful for.

An 'Attitude for Gratitude' as they say, is far more powerful than it seems. I personally have found that it has served me well over the years, particularly for interrupting repetitive worry patterns when the problem is yet to be solved. When that happens, I firstly become conscious of where my focus is right now... in worry mode... then actively choose to think something else. I will make an affirmation statement in my head such as: *'That's enough for now. I am grateful for the lessons I am learning because of my problem, I will find a solution soon.'* Then I create a distraction by thinking about (or saying out loud to myself if I am alone), all the things in my life I AM conscious of being grateful for and say it with love. I find nature to be a perfect distraction and will always raise my spirits. It is impossible not to see the magic going on all around us.

Gratitude is a powerful tool to transform us in many ways, especially when everything is not perfect. We can apply its power during those times when at our lowest, to help raise ourselves up. Sure, it's sometimes hard to feel grateful *for* circumstances and hard times that we really are not enjoying, but it is possible to feel gratitude for the lessons and insight which is coming our way. Yes, gracious in accepting that there are lessons we are receiving through and from our current challenging experiences, as they must be just what we need right now. We learn so much more during our roughest patches, than we do when everything is just hunky dory.

We can also use gratitude to be thankful for those hopes and dreams we are currently wishing into being. The late Dr Wayne Dyer says this:

"You must learn to assume the feeling of the wish fulfilled."

What this means, is simply learning to use the power of our imagination to feel all the positive emotions that would accompany our wish as though it was already fulfilled. Thus, we pretend that 'IT' has already manifested and we are indeed very grateful. This is often the omitted key to working with the Universal Law of Attraction. It is not enough to request what we are hoping for from an abundant Universe, we must also feel in our heart that it has already provided. This is about releasing control over *how* dreams will be fulfilled and instead simply *believing and trusting* that the results we yearn for *will* come to pass in good time.

We are speaking of this in the context of wishing for change that currently may not even seem possible to us. Whilst we believe hold for good. Using such statements diffuses the power of negative words we use and helps draw our attention to our *capability* instead.

See how our thoughts and words can jeopardise positive changes very quickly if we don't become conscious of how we are using them? So let's return to using the power of our imagination to help us to manifest. Think about this in relation at first to those areas which we feel currently could do with some improvement. Is the change needed in personal relationships, career, spiritual exploration, family connections or maybe self belief? We can start by focusing on the way we would like each part of our life to look, and then begin to imagine they are *already like that* without worrying ourselves about *how* they transformed. Tune into the feelings the change has charged within us. We might feel any range of emotions...happy, appreciated, loved, excited, playful, expansive, healthy, calm, confident, empowered, privileged- to name but a few. The key is to imagine the *result of our goal* (not the process of how we got there), then create and hold onto *the feeling it stimulates within us.* This can be done by closing our eyes each day for only five minutes and immerse ourselves in simply imagining our new reality in each area, as though it has already transformed.

This exercise sends a strong intention to the Universe and to our subconscious, that we see ourselves expressing as the happiest and most abundant version of us. In time it *will* come to pass. We can remind ourselves of this vision, whenever we are falling back into a pattern of negative thoughts. For this creative visualisation to be even more powerful, especially when we have difficulties imagining pictures in our mind, it can be easier by doing a calm, relaxed voice recording, speaking about the way our life has now transformed and how this makes us feel. Hearing our own voice confirming our life imagined will make it feel more real and believable. Once our emotions are engaged into that new reality, we can begin to influence the direction our current reality takes for the better. Remember Wayne's words... *'Learn to assume the feeling of the wish fulfilled'.*

Part 2

LIVING FROM THE HEART

∞V.A.V.V.I.∞

VITALITY:

"State of being strong, energetic and active. Exuberant physical strength, mental vigour and capacity for the continuation of a meaningful and purposeful existence."

∞V.A.V.V.I.∞

Chapter 9

OVERCOME YOUR BIGGEST BARRIER-YOU.

*Our body and mind are infused with energy the moment
we realise that we are just as deserving of a wonderful
life as any other human being on this planet.*

When we falter in our belief that we are a good person who is just as deserving as the next, we lose our vital interest and dissolve into living a life which is much like sailing a ship with the sail down. We don't pick up any pace and seem to spend a lot of time not getting anywhere. We don't want the wind to blow, for then we might have to take action and raise our sail! But lo and behold when the wind does pick up, we realise we forgot to pack the sail after all, because we never expected such an opportunity to come our way! That's when the negative mind talk starts and we begin telling ourselves: 'Gee! We always have such bad luck and why is it that everyone else seems to have life so easy and get all the breaks?' The reality is, we are simply in the habit of self-sabotaging any chance of good things happening to us.

Even when we just talk about our hopes and dreams, it can sometimes cause a lot of negative beliefs and fears to begin rising in resistance. We may not even be aware that we are having such thoughts. They can, however, be real enough to block our creative ideas and remind us that we don't deserve to dream big. Our mind may whisper that we aren't capable enough to reach our goals and if we do, such a result will fail to last. These are damaging self-beliefs which will slow us down and even *prevent* our progress towards creating a more meaningful existence. I would like to suggest a great way for you to inject yourself with some renewed faith and self-confidence. Instead of just looking at the areas of life that we need to fix, sometimes we need to *remember the challenges we have already managed to surmount!*

What am I proud of achieving to date?

Acknowledging our prior achievements in all their different shapes and forms can help provide us with the stamina to persevere when things aren't going to plan. We may feel as though there are so many problems to overcome and that we have so far to go to create a life charged with happiness, but why not turn our attention instead to notice *how far we have come?* Many of the obstacles we manage to surmount throughout our life go unnoticed. Every so often however, we could benefit greatly from reminding ourselves of the minor and major 'wins' we've had over the years. This can provide us with a timely injection of both positivity and proud moments!

Positive Reminiscing Exercise:

Break your life up into five year blocks to start with and scan through each period for the major wins that stand out more obviously to you. Then try going back in twelve monthly increments and begin to think about less obvious experiences which, when considered more deeply, have affected you in positive ways. They may have left you wiser, stronger and perhaps even more compassionate as a human being. Don't forget to write your thoughts down or speak them into a voice recorder if you do not like writing. Your experiences do not all have to be obvious successes either, they can be challenges that were hard to get through and may not have necessarily left you feeling on cloud nine post trauma. Hopefully however, you can begin to see that they have each left a unique legacy upon your character, to be appreciated beyond the hardship of the experience.

If you measure your greatness upon that which you don't yet know, then you will never be good enough in your eyes to 'have a go' and become skilled in something different. Measure your greatness instead, by focusing upon that which you already know and have accomplished, so as to remind yourself that you are not only capable, but you are capable of so much more!

This type of self-reflection not only reminds us of the strength and wisdom we have cultivated over the years, but it can also help us to feel more deserving of greater things. There are also actual physiological benefits of remembering such achievements, whereby our body releases feel good hormones when we reminisce about them. This in turn makes it easier to cultivate a positive attitude.

Find that deserving feeling!

We have explored the importance of cultivating a strong why behind taking action, as it helps us feel more confident when confronting fearful emotions of changing our life for the better. So to, it is important that we feel *deserving* of realising our hopes and dreams as well. We may not be conscious of thinking ourselves as being unworthy; it is more likely to be a feeling inside of us which then limits our thoughts and actions. In turn this feeling sabotages our ability to take advantage of opportunity as it comes knocking, just like going for that sail *without* the sail.

Our family, close friends, peer group and the media, all play their part of indoctrinating us with commonly held beliefs about the way life works. This occurs from a young age and often dictates a preference for 'fitting in' and seeking to be the *same as everyone else.* If we have a personality which does not question such information, then we too grow up with these same limiting beliefs ingrained into our subconscious mind. Earl Nightingale once put it this way:

"The opposite of courage is not fear, it's conformity."

One common belief that many of us adopt is that *only the lucky few get to work in an occupation that they absolutely love,* the rest of us just have to accept that life is a 'daily grind'. So if we have the desire to turn an activity we love into work, right from the outset we believe it will be almost an impossible dream. We may also expect to attract disapproval from others.

To overcome such attitudes, firstly we need to have belief in our own capabilities; second, we must be willing to take courageous action; thirdly we must know in our heart that we are deserving of the outcome we seek. Unfortunately many of us find it easier to let the seed of unworthiness set root to ensure we don't even try and conformity seems a much easier option. To this day, I still have conversations with many people who simply do not believe you can succeed in pursuing a hobby as a profession. Artists and musicians are doomed to always hear: 'Why not get yourself a proper job and go scribble on weekends or jam with friends to express your creative bent- following your heart will only make you poor!'

> *"Your first obligation is to carry out the mission you are meant for, not what your father, mother, mate or friends say you should do. Your mission will manifest in you when you decide to listen to your heart's desire."*
> **– Naomi Stephan.**

Once we know what we want, we must then match it with enthusiasm and energetic action. Our committed effort is the only *approval* we need to reach for the stars! Remember though, that just because we are acting in alignment with a heartfelt purpose, does not mean our journey will be easy. We will however, be plugged into such a powerful supply of optimistic energy, that our ability to persist through challenges may surprise us. Such optimism is valuable, for when we dare to be different and seek greater levels of satisfaction from our daily routine, we may become the object of criticism and destabilising attitudes from others. This is based on the premise that sometimes people feel 'shown up' by others who are getting on and doing something that they might have been able to achieve themselves, but lacked the self-belief to do it. Unfortunately, criticising others feels an easier option to them, rather than pursuing the change they want. The famous words of George Bernard Shaw come to mind:

> *"People who say it cannot be done should not interrupt those who are doing it".*

Learning to take action on what we have our heart set upon is a worthy skill and one that takes effort to develop. In fact this ability is *a necessity* when we want to pursue heartfelt, meaningful activities but do not have the approval of those closest to us. Unfortunately when someone doesn't understand our choices, they will often criticise rather than support our decisions. Constructive criticism should be welcomed, but if it is negative criticism just for the sake of it we can recognise it because the person will not genuinely seek to know the reasons behind our decision. There is different forms of criticism too, some are less direct but still undermine our positivity. The person may criticise someone else who is pursuing a similar activity to us; maybe they show disapproving body language when we talk about our intentions or become distracted and change the subject quickly. So whether our 'someone' openly criticises us, or holds their tongue, we are still left with the same feeling that they do not approve.

It helps to understand that criticism and disapproval is not always personal, it is more a reflection of the person's own state of restraint.

> *There are those who will, those who might and those who simply won't. Don't waste your time seeking the approval of the person who closed their mind to the realm of possibility long ago, as it is a closed door that's locked tight.*

Some cultural and religious values may undercut a personal sense of deserving, by limiting pursuits and expectations relative to a person's lineage, gender, age, physical appearance or even state of health. Such beliefs will also influence whether a person even feels they have a right to express their own individual needs or choose their own life direction. Interestingly, there are those who come from such strict cultural beginnings and still they naturally question such restraint imposed by a majority held belief system. This is because they know in their heart, that self-expression and the ability to pursue one's fullest unique potential is a right that belongs to every human being on Earth, not just a select few. These individuals often discover their own unique calling, in speaking up in opposition to the current status quo.

Malala Yousafzai is one such girl. She was only twelve years old when she began her journey as an education activist. She lived in a small town in Pakistan called Mingora in the Swat Valley. Her father was a teacher, committed advocate for education and outspoken opponent of the Taliban's controls to restrict opportunities for education and ban girls from going to school completely. Rather than let the Taliban regime control her future, Malala was inspired to seek to break free of such limitations. With the full support of her father, she began to share the plight of Pakistani women's right to be educated, via Western Nation's media. This led to the Taliban's decision to silence Malala by ordering that she be killed. Fortunately, Malala miraculously survived the single bullet which entered her head, neck and shoulder. However, she required the most specialised care to survive the ordeal, so was flown to the United Kingdom to a hospital in Birmingham which catered specifically to military injuries. By the time she was released several months later, her family had moved to the UK to live in safety. The Taliban received worldwide condemnation for her attempted assassination, which also led to countless protests across Pakistan. In the weeks subsequent to the attack, two million people signed a right to education petition and the National assembly ratified the first Right to Free and Compulsory Education Bill. She and her father have since co-founded the Malala Fund in 2013, to help advocate and empower the millions of girls who are being denied a formal education because of social, political, economic or legal factors. This is how unstoppable a person can be when they have fire in their belly, when they feel driven by a passionate stance, and when they believe with all their heart in the *power* of their intent.

Although it is a really lovely feeling when one feels totally supported by all others around them and the decisions we make are endorsed, it is not realistic to always expect others will agree with what we intend on doing. Neither is it *essential to us succeeding in our pursuits.* In fact the up-side is that it means we must have stronger motivations for staying the course and greater belief in our own ability to persist and that is a *good* thing! Remember, our journey here is to be vibrant, not watered down and put on hold. We are and always should feel, that we are fully deserving to pursue an improved, happier, more fulfilling life, that is bursting at the seams with positive action. To really connect with this belief, we only need spend time centering ourselves in our heart-space each day. This is when we can tap into our personal source of support found deep within our own heart. An infinite supply of love resides there which can provide us with the faith, energy and optimism to carry on through all our tribulations.

HEART CONNECTION MEDITATION

Try doing this for 5-10 minutes each day and see how your inner faith and sense of deserving will blossom. Try reading it slowly and with appropriate pauses, into a sound recorder and play back your voice to provide you with a guided meditation to listen to. As you do this heart meditation, remember to smile and just relax, it is not meant to be hard work, it is meant to be rejuvenating, comforting and loving. When you smile you will soften, de-stress and relax more deeply.

Begin by sitting in a warm and comfortable position. Close your eyes. Become aware of the gentle rise and fall of your chest as with each breath the air regenerates and refreshes your body. Little by little, allow your focus to shift into your heart area. Smile.

Feel your heart pumping tirelessly, generously, holding within it your life force, your energy, it is overflowing with love, gifting your body and mind, movement and thought, feeding every cell, animating every part of you as the blood flows to every part and extremity. Smile.

As you do this, place both your hands over your heart upon your chest, in a relaxed diagonal cross fashion, one on top of the other. Connect with your heart, feel it's movement and gentle persistence- it is your life spark- it makes you the special person that you are, it is the part of you that feels, loves, cares, wonders, knows, believes, connects and holds life's beauty in awe. Smile.

Allow the life force which emanates from your heart as it moves within your chest, to expand- imagine this as a warm pink light that glows from your heart centre. The light is getting bigger with every breath, with every heart beat. The glow is expanding beyond your skin. It is reaching out like a sun shining- warm and comforting. Smile.

This soft pink light is relaxing, it pulsates like a beacon, with its core anchored inside your heart. This soft pink light envelops your whole body and beyond, it protects you and keeps you safe, it supports you, comforts you, and reassures you. Within the glow of this light, you have no doubt, no fear, no negative thought, only feelings of love, optimism and gratitude- life is beautiful and anything feels possible. Smile.

You know that life is special and your heart is the conduit to discover the real you, the YOU that knows how to be happy and to be true to yourself- the YOU that knows what action must be taken and when, the YOU that loves who you are and recognises who you came to earth to be. Smile.

Remain in this state of open awareness for as long as you wish, continuing to feel the ebb and flow of your heart's soft, pink, calming glow. You are happy, you feel assured, you feel supported and most of all you now are aware of the endless source of love which resides within your heart to support you and guide you on your life's journey. Smile, life is wonderful.

The fact is that every single one of us born into this world has innate potential just aching to be expressed. Expressing it is our gift back to the world and inevitably charges us with enduring happiness. If we are challenged with feelings that make us think we are unworthy of a happier, more expressive and fuller life, consider that it is more selfish of us to turn up in life as a lesser version of our true potential.

I like to consider our lives somewhat as the form of a tree...*We each can learn to set down deep, strong, healthy roots into our own knowing of who we are (self-awareness); why we are here (life meaning); and how we best contribute and reach out to the world with the gifts we have (as we give, so shall we receive). Such a strong, enduring root system will be sure to sprout forth a flexible, resilient, healthy body and mind, which will move with winds of change, rebound from times of pressure and grow into its own unique, beautiful form, despite the wildest of weather conditions.*

Self-belief is what enables one to prevail. It allows us to persist beyond every test of strength, stamina, or will. It is the enduring key to build the positive attitude, vitality and inspired vision needed to seek a meaningful life beyond any perceived restraint.

We live in a sea of opportunity, endless ideas and universal abundance, surrounded by instances that we can turn potential into result. It is whether we seize upon the myriad of opportunities that otherwise will simply blow on and pass us by, until they come to rest at the feet of another individual who instead takes action where we did not. Self-belief is a pre-requisite to taking action. Carrying a chip on our shoulder is an assured way that we will behave negatively and attract more negative experiences into our daily activities. Acting selfishly, seeing only the bad in others, expecting the worst, criminal behaviour, treating others in disrespectful ways, allowing others to treat us badly when we deserve so much better... All of these come from feelings of unworthiness and it will ensure that we *do* miss out on better things, mostly as a result of *believing* that we do not deserve to receive all that we need to live life well. But as we discussed in the previous chapter, what we think and verbalise out loud about ourselves can either engage all our abilities and powers to achieve what we set our sights upon, or it can ensure our derailment. So we must overcome any reservations we have inside us, that tell us we are not deserving of a better existence.

We should be critical of ourselves, only if we then tune our focus and energy to positive solutions. For if we acknowledge only the negative and take no positive action, all that we will do is ensure we stay the same, as our focus on what's bad perpetuates its existence...providing the fuel, it's energy to live.

It really is very important that we start noticing the thoughts and words we use repetitively, particularly the thoughts we are having and saying about ourselves. For instance are we telling ourselves how efficient and organised we are, or are we secretly saying 'I am so disorganised and slow as a wet week-can't I pick my game up?' Perhaps when we stare in the mirror and focus on all those attributes we don't like, couldn't we take notice of all the beautiful parts of ourselves instead? Maybe we are constantly plagued by a re-run of a time in our life that we behaved badly and therefore keep telling ourselves that we deserve all the crappy things that happen to us as though it's karmic punishment. When things go wrong we say 'Ohh, that'd be right...that's my luck...I had that coming...everything always turns to S#@T in my life!' Many of us reprimand ourselves regularly when we make a mistake as though we expected and knew we would, by saying 'Erghh! I am such an idiot!'

These constant observations and statements we make about ourselves, our situation and experiences may appear as mostly benign mind babble, but they also have a strong directive influence on our psyche when regularly used. To help turn this around, simply start to notice some of the comments we make, either inside our head or out loud and try to make new comments that have a more positive slant. So for example, if things have just taken an unexpected turn for the worse and you find yourself about to say 'Everything always turns to S#@T!' Try to catch your words mid-sentence and force different words out instead, such as 'Everything always turns out well for me in the end!' There is nothing wrong with spitting it out with emotion either! We can't pretend not to get ruffled about mishaps, mistakes or surprise turns in the road, but we can change the thoughts and words we have about them to support a better outcome, rather than wallow in the terribleness of it all. Tacking on words like 'turns out well for me in the end' is believable, even when you are feeling frustrated. Sure, we all do get handballed some really tough circumstances at some point. But the trick is to try to pass comment as though we are seeing the bigger picture rather than the immediate state of things. This is how optimists live and why things always turn out well for them in the end, because they expect better than what they maybe currently receiving!

Learning to state more positive things and expecting better outcomes, is a great way to get the wheels of acceptance and change turning in our mind. Begin to *entertain the possibility* that you just might be capable, worthy, deserving and loveable after all. We gain most benefit when we say positive affirmations aloud, as it helps to reprogram old negative beliefs that we've been telling ourselves for years. Remember what Mike Dooley said: *"Thoughts become things, but your words are your thoughts that become things the soonest!"*

Affirmations are best when we make them up ourselves in words that we can personally relate to and remember easily. Make them short, positive and present tense, as though the statement is already true. Try to consider how you *intend to be* as though it has already come to pass. So rather than say 'I will try not to be slow and disorganised', better to say:

∞ *I AM efficient, well organised and productive every day* ∞

This is a practice that can be as creative as we wish, or just simple and straight forward if that suits us better. Here are some further random examples:

If you feel uncomfortable accepting compliments from others:

∞ *I now hear and appreciate compliments from others and say thanks* ∞

If you are afraid of change:

∞ *I AM aware that change is safe. I face change with courage and learn the lessons it gifts me* ∞

Maybe you lack self-confidence and feel the need to be more assertive:

∞ *I AM confident and speak my truth easily. I approve of myself* ∞

For someone who wishes to feel more attractive:

∞ *I AM beautiful. I have a beautiful soul and a beautiful body* ∞

Maybe you suffer from nervousness:

∞ *I AM confident and speak my words from the heart. I trust and believe in the goodness of others* ∞

Perhaps you would like to make more positive life choices:

∞ *I feel positive and strong. I listen to my heart-it knows what is best for me. Life is full of new possibilities* ∞

If you are always rushing, feeling as though there is never enough time:

∞ *I AM well organised, there is plenty of time, all is well* ∞

Keep in mind when we create affirmations relevant to our own life and personality, there is much power in using the words 'I AM' as a prelude to any affirmation we create. These two small words state entirely what you *are*, whilst renouncing all that you *are not*. I like to call them the double whammy of positive mind talk.

Chapter 10

STRESS MUST BE FACED, FIXED OR MANAGED.

Stress is one of the biggest barriers to living your most highly vital life, as it robs you of physical energy and mental resilience.

S tress has reached epidemic proportions in our world and it appears to do much more to our body than simply consume our thoughts. When we analyse the connection between stress as a causal agent for many common illnesses and diseases, there appears to be a general consensus on the *range of influence* that stress is considered to have. This figure varies between 75% and as high as 95%. Even within this range, it highlights a considerable impact upon our health. When we ponder such a connection between stress and disease development, we can begin to understand how important it is to control negative stressors in our lives. Even when it does not seem obvious if stress is the primary cause, the odds are, that it *will still be* a contributing factor at the very least.

A healthy body flows from a healthy and happy mind. It is hard to have one without the other. We can have the best diet under the sun, but if we are not dealing with our stress triggers and building up the right positive, resilient mindset, then we will fail in maintaining our natural wellbeing and state of happiness. However likewise, if we don't put the right fuel into our mouths, then both our physical energy reserves and our mental resilience will suffer...but we will talk more about this latter point in the next chapter.

The World Health Organisation predicts that by 2020, depression will rise to become our second highest disease burden affecting people of all ages. Today, depression is already ranked in this category for people between the ages of 15-44 years. They have also stated that there is a definitive correlation for depression to increase the risk for cardiac illness, diabetes, hypertension, whilst also increasing the severity and mortality of any other concurrent medical condition being experienced.[1] In 2013, a health statistics report released from the 33 OECD Nations (Organisation for Economic Co-operation and Development), revealed that Australia is the second highest prescriber of anti-depressant medications in the World, with such prescriptions doubling over the last decade. [2]

Stress is considered a strong precursor to conditions such as chronic anxiety, panic attacks and depression. We are remaining in a state of heightened arousal and tension for long periods of time more than ever before in history. This state is what we call the 'fight or flight response'. Walter Cannon was the first to describe and name this response, back in 1915, noting that it is a response governed by our Sympathetic Nervous System (SNS). This is a natural bodily reaction that occurs in response to perceived 'danger' and also expresses when we start to feel stressed. It served us positively in pre-historic times, when our body diffused the response in a physical way, utilising the hormones and energy productively. It did this by either fleeing predation and aggression; or standing and fighting for our lives. Once the threat was gone, our bodies automatically resumed what is known as the relaxation or 'rest and digest' mode. Now, however, we can be triggered into the fight or flight stress response by a range of mental and physical experiences, as a result of our modern

---

[1] https://www.ncbi.nlm.nih.gov/pmc/articles/PMC3137804/
[2] http://www.abc.net.au/news/2013-11-22/australia-second-in-world-in-anti-depressant-prescriptions/5110084

lifestyles, all of which do not require physical exertion to overcome the stressor and this fact is what indicates we are causing major wear and tear on our body.

There are three main hormones which our body excretes into our bloodstream when under stress: they are cortisol, adrenaline and norepinephrine. All of them have an important role to play in enabling our bodies to become focused and ready for action when under real stress or threat. But when our stress remains chronically constant and uncontrolled, they can have negative side effects on our bodies, which can contribute to debilitating illness, long term. Cortisol for instance, prepares the body for fight or flight by flooding our blood with glucose, supplying an immediate energy source to large muscles, whilst inhibiting insulin production to prevent glucose being stored, to ensure the body has access to quick energy. It also narrows the arteries, while norepinephrine increases the heart rate. Both of these force the blood to pump harder and faster.[3] All fine and dandy when one needs to run from a tiger in pursuit, but not ideal when we have only just arrived at work for the day and already feel our blood pressure rising.

The American Psychological Association also confirms that we have an increased risk of suffering certain health disorders when we are chronically exposed to stress. They have noted that these can include cardiovascular risks such as hypertension, heart-attack or stroke; excessive, chronic muscular tension and pain; increased inclination towards developing diabetes; gastrointestinal disorders such as stomach ulcers, heartburn, reduced absorption of nutrients and over-reactive or sensitive bowels; adrenal fatigue; worsening of allergies and sensitivities; reduced libido and erectile dysfunction; premenstrual syndrome or worsening of menopausal symptoms; and reduced immunity.[4]

Remaining in the 'fight or flight' response actually makes it

---

[3] http://www.todaysdietitian.com/newarchives/111609p38.shtml
[4] http://www.apa.org/helpcenter/stress-body.aspx

impossible for our bodies to release certain bio-chemicals which are known as the feel good, happy hormones- serotonin and dopamine- these are only released once we exit the 'fight or flight' response and slide back into the 'rest and digest' mode. We can only make this transition once we have discharged our stressful feelings by physical exertion or returned to a state of relaxed mental calm. This is why if we don't face, fix or manage the stress we feel, then we become doomed to remain caught on an increasingly anxious and possibly depressed downward spiral, where our body is physically blocking our ability to cope with our daily experiences.

Dopamine is our motivational hormone that helps us to take action towards fulfilling our hopes, dreams and goals. Low dopamine levels result in more procrastination, self-doubt and lack of enthusiasm. Our brain produces dopamine when we do something that then results in positive stimulation, such as gaining a reward. In the hunter-gatherer times this might have been induced by having successfully found shelter when the rain starts falling; or finding a good patch of berries to pick. In our modern day it maybe getting a pay rise; buying a new appliance; or the satisfaction of harvesting home grown vegetables from one's own garden. Even *anticipation* of a reward can release dopamine. This is useful to know... remember Dr Wayne Dyer's advice: *'Learn to assume the feeling of the wish fulfilled.'* If we learn to do this with sincerity and heartfelt trust, our body will not even know the difference! The additional dopamine which is released though will infuse more positive expectation and motivation into our thoughts and actions, supporting our dreams to reach fruition.

Seratonin release, on the other hand, is enhanced when we feel encouraged, significant or important; so we feel like we can have a positive impact and make a difference in our own life or that of others. When one does not feel appreciated, serotonin levels are likely to drop and loneliness and depression can become more prevalent feelings. It is said that reflecting on past significant achievements can allow our brain to re-live the experience and trigger a release of serotonin. Apparently, our brain has trouble distinguishing the difference between what's real and what's imagined, so even creative visualisations can work in the same way. Seratonin release is also supported by nurturing mind and body; so undertaking self care such as having a massage or taking a relaxing bath can help to maintain healthier levels of this powerful bio-chemical. Don't forget the role we play in enhancing our loved ones 'happy hormones' either. They need encouragement and to feel appreciated for what they do in our life, so be prolific in sharing the love and you will be helping to keep others happier and healthier too!

Stress can be a direct or indirect cause of illness. An instance of 'direct' cause could be the development of high blood pressure. As a condition, it does have other causal agents too, but stress is considered one in its own right and if left unchecked, can lead to life threatening heart attacks or stroke. Just because there are other known causes of high blood pressure, does not mean we should any the less consider that stress may be our own main culprit.

An indirect example of stress causing illness is via immune system suppression. Cortisol functions to reduce inflammation in the body. Over time however, chronic inflammation brought on by poor diet choices and the effects of chronic stress will keep cortisol levels raging. Our immune response begins to get out of hand and over-reactive, gradually becoming suppressed, worn out and depleted. This can result in an increased susceptibility to illnesses that normally our bodies would overcome before they take hold. Take the common cold and flu- the more stress we are suffering, the higher the likelihood of us not only coming down with a cold (and any other bug getting around), but also developing additional complications such as ear infections, sinusitis, bronchitis etc. Thus stress can be considered to cause or exacerbate many common complaints. However, the longer our immunity is impaired by unchecked, chronic stress, the greater is its likelihood of allowing development of far graver disorders, such as the now all too common cancer.

It is useful for us to consider our own personal history of complaints and whether they could be attributed to chronic stress; or maybe followed a pattern of emerging to some degree, *after* an acute period of stress. Such symptoms could be allergic reactions, fatigue, migraines, joint and muscle pain; lack of energy, insomnia, muscle tension; brain fogginess, moodiness, acidic reflux; or perhaps coming down with every cold or flu circulating; maybe you feel anxious/ wound up all the time... Of themselves, these symptoms may not exactly feel life threatening, but for those who suffer from them, they know only too well how debilitating they can be. If you could create a life where stress did not get a toe-hold to negatively affect the body anymore, what do you think that would feel like? Peaceful - Calm - Focused - Relaxed. Aaaahh... feels gooood.

When under high levels of stress, our body uses excess amounts of vitamins and minerals to just maintain equilibrium. Magnesium is one of the master minerals that underpins the proper functioning of many bodily processes and is also considered the anti-stress mineral, protecting us from depression, anxiety and generally assisting us to cope more effectively with our ups and downs. In the book "The Magnesium Miracle" written by Dr Carolyn Dean, she discusses the fact that many common drugs such as Statins, Anti-depressants, Antibiotics, Antacids, Anti-inflammatories, Anti-anxiety medications, Antifungals, Steroids, Anti-psychotics (and many more) actually contain Fluoride. She explains that drug companies use Fluoride because it has unique properties which prolong the active presence of the drug in the body. However she also notes: *'While the drug companies may think fluoride is magnifying the effects of the drug, it's also magnifying the number and intensity of the drug's side effects.'* The trouble with Fluoride is that it seeks out minerals such as Magnesium and binds with it, making it unavailable to the body and rendering Magnesium unable to do its work. So this means for those who are taking such medications, their body will gradually become more predisposed to depression and/or anxiety. A whole host of other symptoms can stem from Magnesium deficiency too, such as high blood pressure; diabetes; and chronic inflammation. See how a revolving dependency for some drugs could develop?

In this modern age, we have a tendency to depend on pills to rectify symptoms of illness, without fully taking responsibility for the very *cause* of our symptoms. When a 'cause' is suspected and manageable, I think we owe it to ourselves to take what action we can. Your GP does not always have the time to analyse *why* you have certain symptoms, but they do know that if certain symptoms *continue unchecked* for too long, they can lead to serious effect. Hypertension is certainly one of these. Doctors are also presented with a conundrum- they can recommend certain lifestyle changes to help our symptoms, but have no ultimate control over whether we will make the changes or not. I believe this is what often leads to the prescription of drugs which otherwise could be avoided if the cause was understood better and the prevention options able to be implemented. Being totally honest with ourselves is the best barometer, to recognise if lifestyle choices and/or stress is currently a big influencer upon our health and causing us dis-ease.

Our stress response can be activated, simply by worrying about the future; thinking about a stressful memory from our past; sitting in peak hour traffic; having a disagreement with our spouse; or churning over in our mind negative thoughts too frequently. The key is to *become aware* of those times we are beginning to feel our own unique symptoms of stress response and become our own *stress detective!* We may clench our jaw, purse our lips, slump excessively as though the 'weight of the world' is on our shoulders; tap or pull at our fingers, suffer neck tension and headaches, feel chest tightness, be over-reactive to things said to us; sigh a lot, shallow breathe, experience indigestion or constipation;

lose our temper frequently, or even have a tendency to gain weight or lose weight. The list goes on and on and on. It is important to personalise our list! When we express frustration, become swept up in negative mind talk or feel overwhelmed, try to become more conscious of how the body feels. Our body will always be 'doing' or 'expressing' the stress we feel mentally in a physical way, in our body posture and habits. In fact, such posture is sometimes trying to conceal how one is feeling, trying to keep it inside. That is why we sometimes develop tight muscles as barriers against the outside world penetrating us and become progressively rigid in our mental capacity.

Stress is a gift to help you recognise your problems and deal with them.

Taking the time to get to know what are our own stressors are, provides a tremendous gift of insight. By taking responsibility for and admitting that certain things are causing us stress and strain, then we have the chance to create a fast track way to dispel them and empower ourselves in beautiful ways. Discontent, confusion, frustration and disillusionment are always perched on the cusp of incredible potential for change. However, those same negative emotions can also blind us from seeing the truth, telling us that a 'way out' of our predicament may not exist.

It takes a strong heart to recognise that our current reality is an *imaginary stress trap* which doesn't have to lock us into a path of doom and gloom. We always have options available. Let feelings of stress become our *trigger* for change...a signal that we need to reflect on *why* we feel stressed; *how* we can reduce the stress *without* necessarily changing the situation; then from a calmer place, let our intuition loose to inspire us with *new ways* to solve the primary problem. It is not a sign of weakness either if we want to remove ourselves completely from a situation which is very stressful to us... it is wisdom!

Remember in Chapter 4 when we discussed the value of clarifying problems and to stop pretending they don't exist? Well that is exactly the way to overcome debilitating effects of stress...*admit to having a problem* first. Second, we work to lessen the effects of stress by undertaking *consistent stress reduction activities*. Lastly, make a decision to *love and honour ourselves*. If we do this, we will make space for taking actionable steps towards whatever change we need to create a more positive place to enjoy living.

Are your current priorities in tune with what you consider to be most important?

Often our stress can develop from an altered or mal-aligned sense of priorities, because what one person considers most important to do, have, be or express, is very different to another. The *Strategic Intervention* philosophy, explains that we are all motivated by six human needs: Certainty; Significance; Love and Connection; Variety; Growth; and Contribution. Out of all these human needs as individuals, we attach a higher importance to at least two in relating to our world around us. Which ones we prioritise can also alter as the years pass. Out of those two that we deem presently most important, we will additionally elevate one of them above the other as well. This helps explain how we are all motivated in slightly different ways.

For instance, two people may share the same two top priority needs- Love and Connection and Certainty. But the point of difference will be in which one they choose to elevate above the other one. So let's say the first person considers Love and Connection is important above the need for Certainty, whereas the second person definitely prioritises Certainty over Love and Connection. So how does this affect their motivational drives, emotions, pursuits and desired outcomes in different areas of their life? Well, the first person will seek out more opportunities to *express and receive* Love and Connection in *their pursuit* of Certainty. Whereas the second person will seek to *establish* Certainty *before* they can be fully comfortable expressing and receiving Love and Connection. Can you see the big difference in motivation? Then consider how these *need priorities* may affect various life areas such as: Work; Relationships; Personal self-worth; Family; or Community.

To provide some examples for the above two people...In a workplace, the first person may find themselves trying to be everyone's best friend or they may feel lack of fulfilment in a job which is isolated and disconnected from people, because their innate need is to feel connection with other people. The second person may find career satisfaction only once they feel irreplaceable in their position, as this provides them with the job certainty they desire as a precursor to connecting better with other staff members. The first person may seek out more loving support from a spouse when experiencing financial insecurity, as it assures them their relationship is strong and they can get through any challenge; whereas the second person may withdraw from the loving relationship they have until the financial strain is over. Can you see how our subconscious need priorities can cause big voids in close relationships if not fully understood?

The need that we make top priority has a huge impact on the way we relate to everyone else and will drive our motivations in every life area. If we do not recognise which of these six needs we inwardly prioritise first, then we will remain in a state of confusion as to why we feel discontented and unfulfilled. If we learn to understand what priority need is motivating those we are in close relationship with, then we can begin to recognise that their actions towards us are not necessarily personal, but rather a direct attempt to express and fulfil that particular need for them right now. This knowledge can assist us to be more tolerant of other's behaviours and it can also enable us to be more conscious of why we do what we do. Ultimately however, understanding what our own personal priority need is right now, can really help us to gain insight into what area of our life really could do with a makeover if we are to feel more highly motivated and be happier individuals.

Chapter 11

HEALTHY BODY, HEALTHY MIND.

*Step into your power, appreciate the benefits of
good health, and take good care of the vehicle
you are travelling through life in.*

Respecting one's body, enhancing our natural good health and vitality, is paramount to becoming inspired and creative. We block our heart's creative ideas when we have no extra energy to follow through with action. We have started to explore the mind/body connection in understanding stress symptoms. As we now know, taking responsibility for our problems, pro-actively choosing better options and cultivating a more positive perspective is really important in our pursuit of calmer living. We have acknowledged the physical imprint that mental stress can have on us and how it can take its toll on our mindset, energy levels and rob us of good health. Our mind can certainly keep us trapped in a stressed state, however, lucky for us, it is really possible to help lower our stress levels and improve our mechanism to cope, by modifying our current lifestyle habits to take good care of our physical body, balance our bio-chemistry and optimise our healthy brain function.

If our bodies do not receive the right daily fuel, nutrition falls short and our nervous system's reserves run low. This depletion reduces our body's ability to respond to stress triggers in a calm, tolerant way, especially when we are enduring circumstance which are pressing our buttons constantly. Existing on fast food; incorporating a lot of processed ingredients in meals we create; will result in nutrient deprivation of the vitamins and minerals our body requires daily to operate efficiently. There is much research which now tells us that most of our soils which grow our fresh food are depleted in minerals. This is largely because traditional farming practices tend to seek the highest returns from artificially high levels of productivity, in the shortest span of time. They can do this by using fertilisers which are fast release, supplying nutrients to their crops in a highly absorbable form. The objective is to deliver nutrient directly as plants are growing, using the soil more like a hydroponic medium, rather than achieving long term, progressive soil conditioning and improvement. There develops a progressive dependency on chemicals and genetic alteration to control weeds and pest insects, because the plants are not as robust, or able to compete with their more vigorous weedy companions.

Organic and biodynamic farming practices treat the soil like our own body- a living breathing system that has its own methods of maintaining good health, if given the right building blocks of essential nutrients in a natural, wholesome form. The soil itself then becomes a living medium, host to millions of microbial bacteria, earthworms and other insects which all play their own part to strengthen plants natural immunity and vigour. Our bodies are just the same, we cannot build a strong immune system or be mentally resilient, by existing on foods that have been denatured, highly processed and then had some synthetic vitamins and minerals 'put back in' in an attempt to provide us with those nutrients that were taken out! In nature's produce, there are complex combinations of enzymes, vitamins, minerals, proteins, essential fatty acids and many other goodies, which we will never be able to re-create artificially, let alone ever achieve the same health benefits from. So a wholesome, organic, primarily fresh food diet is the first way we heighten our ability to be healthier and happier. Even made better if we can grow some of our own fresh fruit and vegetables, as not only does this give us direct control over our growing methods, to ensure our plants are naturally well mineralised and grown organically, but it also provides us with exercise- another powerful way to help treat mental stress, from endorphins we release during physical activity!

Reduction of processed sugar and carbohydrates is also worth making a special mention, as it has a particularly strong influence upon our mental stability. There are numerous studies showing the direct correlation between elevated blood sugar levels (brought on by a high intake of highly refined processed foods and sugary drinks) and a person's tendency to be depressed. The reason for this is that processed foods lead to quick unsustained peak release of glucose, which leads to emotional highs and quick energy, closely followed by a rapid drop in glucose, energy and mood also. To help stabilise one's mood swings, we must also stabilise our blood sugar levels. Consuming a wholesome diet as was noted previously, rich in complex carbohydrates, natural fibre, fruit, vegetables, healthy fats and simple proteins, is an essential part in the puzzle to reduce your stress load. Skipping meals is a no-no also, because we tend to make up for missing a meal at the next one by eating more than we should; or snacking on food that is a quick fix (salty, sugary) and once again, our glucose levels will be on a rollercoaster ride and so too will our brain!

We are what we drink as well. Drinking plenty of pure water to remain hydrated- 2 litres at least per day over and above other forms of liquid- is essential to ensure nutrient freely moves around our body to where it is needed. It will also ensure that our food gets digested properly and toxins are efficiently released from the body. Research tells us that 75% of the American population is in a state of chronic dehydration[5]. Grace Webb, Assistant director for clinical Nutrition at New York Hospital was quoted as saying *"People just think that when they start to get a little weak or they have a headache, they need to*

---

[5] http://www.medicaldaily.com/75-americans-may-suffer-chronic-dehydration-according-doctors-247393

eat something, but most often they need to drink. Problem is, because the human body is so unique, it will say 'I want water, in any way, shape or form'. "Of course just *any form* is not good enough if we are to thrive long term, not when our bodies are composed of 25% solid matter and the remaining 75% is made up of water! Brain tissue has an even higher component of water, 85% in fact. Interestingly, quite a lot of people I talk to are under the misconception that drinking any liquid is automatically hydrating the body, but this is simply not the case. Caffeinated drinks for instance, especially coffee, doesn't result in a net gain of hydration for the body, as it will use some of the liquid as a natural part of digesting the drink and the rest unfortunately get's expelled due to the diuretic effect of the caffeine.

Dr Mark Sircus, in his article: "Dehydration. Symptoms, causes and treatments",[6] emphasises that second only to oxygen deprivation, dehydration robs life the fastest. He says that our cells are made of water and they live in a water solution. Our blood is mostly water and serves to transport nutrients and eliminate waste materials. When dehydrated the blood becomes thick and saturated and is unable to flow freely. Excess toxins become stored in the space surrounding our cells, over time becoming like a toxic acidic waste dump, which then prevents healthy exchange of nutrients and oxygen to the cell. Whenever our body cannot deliver nutrients to cells or carry away metabolic wastes, we set up the conditions for disease.

It appears that the intake of pure water with a little added mineral salts, can be the most hydrating to the body. Once again we revisit the benefit of Magnesium, which as Dr Norman Shealy says *'Magnesium is the most critical mineral for electrical stability of every cell in the body. A Magnesium deficiency maybe responsible for more diseases than any other nutrient.'* When we add magnesium chloride to water (which is one of the more absorbable forms of magnesium), it increases the hydrating effect of the water in our body, helping to maintain the

---

[6] http://drsircus.com/medicine/water/dehydration-symptoms-causes-treatments

right blood viscosity, nutrient balance and relaxes the blood vessels, thus it can be used as a helpful preventative against hypertension, stroke and heart disease.

In his book '*Your Body's Many Cries for Water*', Dr Batmanghelidj says that dehydration causes high blood pressure, because when the body is even slightly dehydrated, it attempts to hold onto whatever water it can by constricting blood vessels throughout the body. You sweat less and lose less moisture when you breathe. The effects of even mild dehydration include decreased co-ordination, confusion, fatigue, dry skin, decreased urine output, dry mucous membranes, blood pressure changes and impairment of judgement. Dr B. maintains that stress, headache, migraines, back pain, allergies, asthma and many other degenerative health problems can be the result of what he likes to term as unintentional chronic dehydration (UCD). He goes so far as to say that: '*Chronic pain of the body which cannot be easily explained as injuries or infection should first and foremost be interpreted as signal of chronic water shortage in the area where the pain is registered. These pain signals should first be considered and excluded as primary indicators for dehydration of the body before any other complicated procedures are forced on the patient. To hush the body's call for water by masking the symptoms with drugs, is like turning out the dashboard light that signals us that our car is about to overheat.*'

It makes sense to first consider the most simple of cures, whether we are getting enough hydration into our body, before turning to medications and complicated treatments to fix our ailments. Interestingly, lack of water could really be one of the most underestimated causal factors of ill health in our society. It appears the busier we are and the more pre-occupied with our stressors, problems and timelines, the less likely we are to be listening to our body's signals that it is thirsty for the liquid that revitalises and hydrates...pure water. An easy habit that I would encourage all of us to do, is to have a big glass of water before any other liquid. We do not necessarily have to go without another preferred beverage that is inefficient at hydrating our body, such as tea, coffee, or alcohol; but we can try to adopt the habit of drinking water first. We can take a bottle of water with us wherever we go and simply develop the pattern of drinking from it before we partake of other liquids! If the taste of pure water is non-preferred, just add a squeeze of lemon, fresh fruit pieces or make a natural herbal tea and cool in the fridge for later. Don't forget to try adding magnesium chloride flakes to water, as this will also help alter the taste a little and increase the hydrating ability of water in our body.

Sleep and good ol' R & R.

Getting plenty of regular sleep and rest is very important to managing our stress levels and physical wellbeing. Although everybody is different, most people will not function well without at least 6-8hrs sleep every night. Our body repairs itself when in sleep mode and processes a lot of emotions we feel throughout the day. Our mind needs to switch off every night to reset for the next day. After a good night's sleep, emotional discord we may have felt the day before will never seem so intensely bad the next morning, until we consciously start 'feeding' it with emotive thoughts again.

The Division of Sleep Medicine at Harvard Medical School[7] has recognised the important role that sleep plays in our lives. They have undertaken a variety of research studies to increasingly understand both the benefits of sleep and the repercussions of sleep deprivation to an average human being. This ongoing research is proving that we are at a greater risk of developing a number of different chronic diseases and health problems if we do not get adequate, good quality, sleep. We all know how ordinary we can feel after just one bad night's sleep- feeling fatigued, grumpy and experience a much reduced ability to concentrate.

One such sleep study undertaken at Harvard on healthy research

---

[7] https://sleep.med.harvard.edu/

participants, exposed the volunteers to sleep deprivation. This has revealed a variety of potentially harmful side-effects and short-term physiological changes that are known possible triggers for disease. Most of which are associated with increased levels of stress, such as high blood pressure, more reactive inflammatory response and impaired control of blood glucose. Basically, if we are not getting enough sleep on a regular basis, we increase the chance of developing or worsening an underlying condition such as: heart disease, hypertension, depression, anxiety, mental stress, erratic mood swings, impaired immunity, diabetes and weight gain. Poor sleeping habits are also associated with an overall lowered life expectancy, which comes as no surprise! In fact, sleeping for five hours or less per night increased mortality risk from all causes by approximately 15% according to further Harvard sleep studies.

It is not the intention of this book to get bogged down in statistical evidence, but the truth of the matter is that every person can benefit from seeking out information for themselves. I have felt it important to emphasise the impact that sleep, or lack of, has on our state of health, peace of mind and life motivation. We often complicate stuff more than we should, underestimating the impact that some of our most basic life habits have long term, on our wellbeing. If we suffer from an underlying condition that causes us a lack of sleep on a regular basis, don't ignore or accept such sleep deprivation. It is possible to assist ourselves sleep more soundly by discovering natural enhancers of good sleep and to figure out the real reason for our wakefulness. Unresolved problems can be a huge stimulant at night, quickly busying our brain the minute we wake up, when we would much rather be asleep.

Many people think of alcohol as having relaxing qualities and maybe surprised to know that alcohol actually contributes only to poor sleep patterns. The reason for this, is that alcohol is mildly sedating at first, increasing our chances of initially falling off to sleep, but this effect is short lived. Alcohol gets processed in the body over the course of a few hours, by which time arousal receptors in the brain then begin to be stimulated, causing wakeful episodes throughout the night, resulting in poor quality sleep. There can be many contributors to insomnia and sub-standard sleep routines. Some prescribed medications may have the undesirable side-effect of inducing insomnia in susceptible users; chronic pain can be a major culprit for others; restless legs syndrome can prevent some from solid sleeping habits (a condition that I have seen improve remarkably by the way, just by re-mineralising the body); too much caffeine consumption late in the day; late night screen starers may wonder why they switch off technology and then can't switch off their brain; whilst too much electromagnetic radiation bouncing around our bedroom from the same, can interfere with a sound sleep as well. In other words, switch off Wi-fi modems at night, charge up mobile phones away from our sleep space (or at least switch to aeroplane mode) and strictly limit television and computer use before bedtime. Your bedroom should be reserved only for sleep, relaxation or relaxed exertion...did you know that TV and computer usage in the bedroom is one of the most well known antagonists to lovemaking? Do we really want to be distracted from a completely natural physical activity which not only feels awesome, but ensures the release of relaxing, feel good endorphins that help us to sleep more soundly?

Developing a night time ritual can do wonders to overcome a resistant mind from switching off. Having a late night shower or bath; diffusing relaxing essential oils into the air of our bedroom at the same time each night, or dabbing a relaxing blend onto temples/pillow; enjoying a herbal tea blend before bedtime with any of the following- chamomile, valerian, lavender, peppermint, passionflower, lemon- balm. The trick is to create habits which are then associated as 'wind down time'. Any stress relief method like meditation, mindfulness, progressive muscle relaxation or listening to beautiful, relaxing music before bed-time can work wonders too.

It is also fair to consider that sometimes we can get *too much* sleep. This can happen when we feel mentally exhausted and all we can think of is falling into bed, but in fact if we go to bed too early, we can also become wakeful later in the night, whereupon our brain 'kicks in' again trying to solve all our issues. Mental exhaustion can come from being over-stimulated by stress, problems, and generally excessive mind work, with not enough physical expression of the energy created mentally. That's when relaxing wind down routines can certainly come into their own to help us feel a conscious sense of *switching off* from our day's heavy mental focus. This then leads us to the next important catalyst maintaining our vitality...

Physical exercise.

The impact that physical exertion and exercise has upon our state of mind is grossly underestimated by a lot of people. It is one of the most natural ways to disperse stress and tension which builds up during our day. It is particularly helpful for people who find themselves in daily environments where they cannot express the tension that builds up in a physical way as they feel it. Our fight or flight stress response, will naturally reset itself back into a relaxed state once we have expended energy. Historically, that is how our nervous system was built to work back in the hunter/gatherer time, our mind and body experienced pressure, stress, an adrenalin rush, brought on by having to confront a threat or run from one. Either way we expended energy doing so, then once the threat was over, we returned to the relaxed, rest and digest mode.

What is the best form of exercise? The one that *you do*! It does not need to be formal like going to the gym. Just going for a regular walk or digging weeds out in the garden for a sustained period of half an hour is great! Taking regular exercise in the open air is extremely helpful to our state of mind, particularly for example, in breaking up our stressful work day periods whenever possible. This serves the purpose of changing our environment, providing our body and mind with fresh oxygen, stimulating our thinking and helping to change our mental focus. Exercise releases endorphins which help us to feel more relaxed, happier and energised. Just going for a 5-10 minute walk can work wonders. In addition to this, partaking of other regular exercise habits that last for 30 minutes, three times a week is equally important, but choose to make it something you enjoy and look forward to. The euphoria of a 'runners high' during and after a vigorous run is the result of endorphin release. It can also help as an analgesic and sedative, diminishing our perception of pain and making us feel like we are invincible. However, personally I can get the same happy, relaxed, invigorated feelings from going for a lively walk through a beautiful place in nature, as I feel stimulated physically *and* mentally by what I observe going on around me. This is why it is important for our choice of exercise to resonate with what we enjoy, as we are more likely to stick with it as an ongoing life habit, not just start off on a fitness kick and drop it after one week.

A smile goes a long way.

Along with exercise, laughter is the next best way to enhance endorphin release in our body, so don't underestimate the benefits of having a good ol' belly laugh. Instead of a scary thriller, consider choosing a tummy tickling comedy! Sebastian Gendry is an international expert in laughter and wellness and has created an interactive practice known by the same name - *The Laughter Wellness Method*.[8] He likes to share some interesting facts about our smiles, a few of which I would like to share with you now.

---

[8] http://www.laughteronlineuniversity.com/sgendry/

❖ *Smiling builds a stronger immune system.* Our body becomes more relaxed when we smile, which as we know, is essential to maintaining good health and stimulating our immunity.

❖ *Smiles are contagious.* In a study conducted in Sweden, people had difficulty frowning when they looked at other subjects who were smiling and in most cases shifted into a smile as well.

❖ *Smiles relieve stress.* Our body immediately releases endorphins when we smile, even when you force it!

❖ *Smiling helps us get promoted.* Smiles make a person seem more attractive, engaging and confident, thus people who are inclined to smile more often are likely to get a promotion over someone who does not!

❖ *Smiles are more attractive than make-up.* A research study undertaken by Orbit Complete, discovered that 69% of people find women more attractive when they smile, than if they are wearing make-up.

No matter whether we believe in laughter practice as an important part of stress reduction, for when we are feeling genuinely happy and relaxed, laughter becomes a very natural and spontaneous form of expression. If we are not laughing much, take this a serious indicator that we need to embrace some positive change.

Methods to help manage and disperse the build up of stress each and every day.

It is necessary to take action every day, to disperse the effect that stress wreaks on our body and mind. Good nutrition, exercise, plenty of sleep and drinking adequate amounts of water, are all certainly essential ingredients in doing this. However, there are other activities we can undertake to help us feel happier, a great deal more relaxed and further reduce our stress load. Meditation has been proven to be one of the most effective ways to help us to do this. It also assists us to maintain an easier state of calm as we move through our daily tasks and challenges, when we adopt it as a regular habit of even just ten minutes per day. It is the ability to balance our resilience as well as negate our tendency to over-react to events, that I think makes meditation so powerful. Basically, it helps us to cope better with whatever life throws at us.

Unfortunately, meditation by some is considered only an activity aligned with religious beliefs, but this is simply not so. Nor is there really a right or wrong way to undertake meditation. It does not have to be rigid in practice, but can fit into and around other activities we do daily. Meditation can be undertaken whilst sitting down, completely still, eyes closed in complete silence; or we can listen to music or guided visualisations to help give the mind a focus point; or we can sit with eyes open in quiet observation, concentrating on one thing like a candle burning in front of us. I personally love *active* forms of meditation where we practice a conscious mindfulness, emptying our mind of busy thoughts and keep refocusing upon only that which we can sense in the given moment. This type of meditation can be used whilst walking in a peaceful environment or whilst listening to music and dancing. The objective is to keep bringing our awareness back to the present moment, training our brain to dismiss past and future thoughts. The main intention with any form of meditation is to slow down random brain talk and give our head a break from the incessant busy thoughts that keep us stuck in a heightened state of stress.

As stress also builds up in our physical body, it is also valuable to consider doing a daily progressive muscle relaxation exercise to help release tension that exists in our muscles. The objective of PMR is to help train our mind to become more conscious of tension and with practice, be able to release this muscle tightness on command. I have personally found that undertaking a stretching routine is beneficial as a prelude to PMR, even if just initially, for it helps us to become more conscious of the main muscle groups which are holding most of our tension. Not to mention that regular stretching exercise certainly has its valued place to help our bodies remain flexible, priming us for our daily activities and reducing the likelihood of injury.

Yoga has become a very popular activity and is frequently undertaken by many for its myriad of health benefits. This can include stress reduction, enhancement of physical flexibility, core strength, dispersal of muscular tension, support of both physical/ mental wellbeing and general longevity. Tai chi, Pilates and Qi Gong are also other activities which are great for our body as well as reducing stress and tension of the mind. It is important to point out, however, that the medium of delivery for undertaking any relaxation activity is essentially important. Many people choose to attend classes, but if this means dealing with peak hour traffic to get there, battling through the crowd of participants just to get a decent spot in class, or missing out on a class regularly due to other commitments which clash, then perhaps any benefit gained (for stress-relief) will be lost. It may be better to consider going to classes long enough to learn the basics, but then carry on in the comfort and peace of home, perhaps with a DVD for guidance. Each of us must be the judge of our own situation and gauge which option will bring us the greatest benefit.

There are many different ways to assist lessen the effects of stress upon our mind and body. It is important to choose activities which resonate with our heart and naturally seem to attract us, rather than to please someone else or is currently 'trending'. Some can be interspersed throughout our work day as we feel tension and others maybe best done at home or other location of our choosing. Remember that doing anything is better than *nothing*. Keep in mind that stress builds up in a static body more quickly than one that moves because it has nowhere to go; it just sits inside us, steadily building up, tightening our muscles and mind. To move, means our energy get's shifted, it get's expressed and used in a moving body, which both invigorates and at the same time relaxes.

Creative expression is a great form of relaxation too, so perhaps we should stop putting off learning to play that musical instrument; write that novel; express ourselves on canvas; craft that sculpture; or design that new garden feature? When we express our creative side, we become immersed in what we are doing as it is an active form of mindfulness therapy... living in the moment.That is why adult colouring books have become such a hit, they provide a convenient version of creative expression and opportunity to screen out all the 'life noise' but without any added pressure to learn new skills! For some this is more appealing than learning the art of drawing, if so, then go for it. We don't all need to be Vincent Van Goghs!

There are so many different ways with very little time required, which we can help to calm ourselves and discharge stress, so there really should not be any excuse for not doing *something* in our day. Music can be a powerful agent for inducing a relaxed state of mind. Downloading a few serene music tracks onto our mobile phone means it's possible to tap into a five minute break of relaxing music immersion whenever we have the need. If we love gardening, then come home from work and spend fifteen minutes weeding, pruning, digging, planting; or maybe just sit outside under a tree soaking it all in. If the beach is our thing, why not go for a nice walk on the sand, or drop a rod in to catch a fish for dinner. We must be guided by what genuinely feels right for ourselves... our heart knows what we need, we just need to listen.

Don't forget to breathe.

Rejuvenating rest, relaxation and recreation, is as essential as the air we breathe. But becoming more conscious of our breathing deserves a mention here too. When we are feeling uptight and stressed we often shallow breathe. That means we refrain from really opening our chest to take a nice deep breath into our lungs and out, which just adds to the tightness we feel. That's why exercise is a great change to one's state, as it forces us to breathe in oxygen deeply, consciously or unconsciously, whether we like it or not! Here is a gentle breathing activity that we can do at anytime throughout our day in a quiet, private space - it is called 'Butterfly breathing'.

Butterfly Breathing Technique

Begin by standing with your back straight and your feet slightly apart, flat upon the ground or floor. Let your arms drop by your sides, relaxed. Then bring your hands into a softly crossed position in front of your sternum and exhale fully. Allow your hands to drop away gently to your sides and into an extended stretch outwards as you begin to inhale slowly and deeply into your abdomen and chest. Your arms will move fluidly, fully extended, floating in a rounded arc from down near your sides as though you are unfurling your wings and raising your arms and hands up on either side of your body, raising them ever upwards until the backs of your hands come together above your head. Pause and continue to stretch skywards. Your breath should have been long and slow to match the slow raising of your arms into the fully extended position above your head. After your brief pause, begin to exhale as you return your arms (your wings) down in the same way you went up, bringing them back to rest, crossed in front of your sternum again softly. Pause for a few seconds before repeating again by inhaling as you raise both arms up extended fully outwards and upwards to above your head- stretch upwards- pause, then exhale back to the starting position, hands crossed in front of sternum. Do this for about ten repeats. Your breathing should not be forced or held for too long- it can be useful to count as you inhale, then count to the same as you exhale, making the in and out breath equal.

∞V.A.V.V.I.∞

VISION:

"State of being able to See, power of sight. The ability to think about and plan the future with imagination and wisdom."

∞V.A.V.V.I.∞

Chapter 12

WHAT REALLY MATTERS?

"The World is but a Canvas to the Imagination."
– Henry David Thoreau.

Every 'thing' has its origin in thought. If we learn to be courageous enough to let loose our imagination, we will develop much greater certainty about what we long to create out of this lifetime. Most of us don't really know what we *do* want from life. Generally it seems easier to have a clearer picture about what we don't want! When we fall into the category of not yet knowing, the following series of questions can really help define our goals, hopes and desires beyond that which we do from day to day if we are not fully engaged and enjoying what we presently do. Our happiness depends upon it. We know that we can perceive the good from whatever circumstance we find ourselves, but that does not mean we cannot play an active hand in moulding our future.

As we get older, we forget to see the world as if for the first time, with fresh, new vision. I know that when I was in my teens, it was so easy to see the magic and exciting potential that was held in store for me...anything seemed possible. But as the years pass and not everything works out quite as we imagine, it is easy to expect less and judge more. This is normal, in fact some would term this stage 'older and wiser', but it also comes with the risk of losing sight of our dreams. Here is the kicker... cynicism does not generally lead to happiness, only self-righteousness. It reduces the amount of new information we take on board and prevents us seeing things from a different perspective. Thinking we have all the answers and always know best, is dangerous territory, as it camouflages our creative imagination, dismissing ideas as unrealistic and unachievable.

When we really want to get to the heart of what matters to us, we need to reconnect with the child that still resides within. The one that's still excited about the possibilities and adventures that lie ahead, rather than feels bitter about lost opportunity from the past. The child that still enjoys the little simplicities- the magic in a sunrise; the invigoration of walking in the rain; the delicious aroma of freshly baked bread; and the warm embrace of a loved one. We should not get complacent about what our existence offers to us, even when it does so every single day without fail. Consider instead, that every day is a new day and new experience. We can choose to embrace opportunity; appreciate and notice what is going on around us; and believe that we can make a difference in the world, just like we probably thought when we were eighteen years of age. Knowing that we can do this at any time, means that 'now' will always be the best time to take action on the path of our dreams.

When considering our goals, dreams and desires, we know how important it is that they align with heartfelt personal values and ethics. If we try to act in ways which are not in tune with our values, we meet with a lot of internal resistance in fulfilling those goals and will be likely to make slow or no progress at all. So in setting out to achieve a purposeful and passionate intention, we must align fully with our ethics, otherwise our heart will seek to be heard and derail our activities.

The following questions have been designed to help attune us to such values and open our mind to those elements which help make our life seem more meaningful. This in turn helps reveal new paths for us to explore positive change. Please do take however long you need to answer them honestly. If that is twenty minutes for you, that's great- but if it is two weeks, then *that is the time you need to self-reflect.* Whatever amount of time you invest will repay you a thousand times over in providing you with more clarity going forward. It is important to note here too, that before you answer the following questions, you need to cast aside the voice of doubt, fear or past regret. You are not simply the sum of your parts. You are not who you were in the past and you are not your present circumstance, (however limiting it may seem right now), nor do you have to be trapped by your current mindset. The past has been and gone and the circumstance and mindset you currently have can be changed in a heartbeat. So with that in mind, open up to your fullest potential and dare to imagine your absolute best existence. Let yourself tap into the wisdom of your heart, which already knows what you would most love to experience.

1) What do you love to do? What are your interests, hobbies or activities that make you feel happiest when you spend time doing them? Also consider what subjects you love learning or reading about.

2) What do you long for? Do you romanticise over some possible change/outcome that up until now you have discounted? Consider a 'longing' as the opposite to any discontent or frustration you may currently feel. It may be the solution and alternate path away from an issue that is causing you pain right now.

3) If you had no possibility of failing, were aware of no personal restraints and were guaranteed success, what would you choose to do?

4) What do you imagine your most ideal day would look like? (Remember we would all get very bored if we did nothing, all day every day on a holiday in the Bahamas...sure, go for a holiday, get some much needed R and R and then come home and decide how you want to spend your days between holidays!) What time would you get up; where do you live; what work would you choose to do; what could you do for others that would make you

feel happy and fulfilled? Do you have a hobby that you wish you could be paid to work at? Are there specific daily activities that you consider share equal priority with, or even greater status, alongside your income producing activities?

5) When you are at your most happiest, what would you consider your most positive personality traits to be? Remember, if you are currently lacking some zest for life, think back to a particularly wonderful time in your past and reflect on who 'that' was and how 'they' behaved. Are you a larrikin, conversationist, loving, empathic, passionate, expressive, creative, energetic, inspired, inventive, persistent, a little crazy and adventurous, fun-loving, thoughtful, a dreamer, an action taker, courageous, reflective, kind and considerate- you get the point!

6) What would you do now if you believed the world would end in a year from now? What is so important to you that you would waste no time in doing it, learning more about it, sharing or teaching it?

7) What do you consider are your natural abilities/strengths? These are those qualities that are second nature to you, rather than skills you have worked hard to build and retain. You may think of them as special quirks or eccentricities, or areas of passion/ talent. They may have been intensified through your life experience or naturally enhanced from that which you have learnt, but generally come easy to you and are not forced skill. Are you currently using these productively or have you discounted them as unimportant?

8) What matters most to you at your core and makes you feel passionate? What topics can you talk about with others until 'the cows come home'? What sort of issues upset you the most? Sometimes those issues you have a high level of empathy and concern for may trigger your defence in conversation or even spark a difference of opinion in your relationships. This indicates they are heart centred values and very important to you.

9) If you think about a person you really admire, why is that? What qualities do they have that makes you hold them in high regard, look up to them or listen to what they have to say?

10) Cast your mind back to when you were a teenager...was there anything you felt excited about and was looking forward to doing when you came of age? Did you do it- if so, has it fulfilled you as you imagined? If you did not pursue the path you intended, why do you think this was? In your opinion now, did you happen to find a life and career path as equally fulfilling and enjoyable as you had hoped for?

11) Have you felt 'blocked' from taking positive action by some recurring thing? It could be something internal, such as a belief about yourself; or external, such as an unresolved issue involving someone else. It maybe a negative circumstance or thing in your life you feel captive to, or that you have no choice over. This is not to be negative, it is to name the 'elephant in the room' which surprisingly could be a source of inspiration for your future if you can face and fix this problem.

12) What does it mean to you to feel truly healthy? What would you need to be doing differently do you think, to feel that ideal level of health? In other words, do your current daily habits support you to be your most healthy version or not?

13) If you were to earn a high consistent income, doing something you really enjoyed, how would you choose to spend that money? How would it positively influence your life? Would others benefit from your wealth? Would your dreams and goals be different do you think? In what way?

14) Move forward five years from now, in what ways would you like to see things change for the better? What would you be doing or have done that is different to what you are doing now? How has that affected the way you look upon your life experience? What lessons have you learnt? How do you feel about yourself because of the changes?

15) Have you ever fantasized about how you could make the world a better place- is so, how?

16) Now move forward in time to that moment you are lying on your death bed, you have no regrets, you have lived a full life. What has happened over the years that you feel most fulfilled by- it may help to break this down further into such areas of your life- family; career; community; relationships; and personal. What do you reflect on that has injected your life with meaning and provided you with the most happiness? What contribution have you made during your lifetime that has given you the greatest level of satisfaction? What do you consider is your legacy to others?

Hopefully these questions, if answered honestly and in no rush, will help you to get more deeply in touch with your own motivations and values, hopes and desires, without your judgemental intellect getting in the way. Your heart pushes you to express as your authentic self always, so any goals worth striving towards need to genuinely resonate with that which you value *if the change is to last*. This self-awareness will stand you in good stead as you explore and decide on the most worthy ideas to be at centre stage of your future life vision.

Chapter 13

DITCH THE PROCRASTINATION!

"You can't have life vision for the future, when your head and physical surroundings are cluttered with yesterday's mess."

To be a clear channel for us being our most imaginative and inspired selves, we first need to rid ourselves of old modes of being, unsolved problems and clutter from other times in our life. This creates a clean slate for inviting new positive experience and increases our inclination to do things differently from how we may have done them in the past.

Is your 'To-do' list as long as the Great Wall of China? Maybe you have been brooding on certain ideas for longer than you care to admit without taking any action. Having distractions come at us from inside and outside our head is not conducive to being at our most productive. There is an invisible force at work here, preventing us from being the most effective and energetic person that we can be. Procrastination with a big 'P' is one of the most common limiting factors that impose on our lives.

We often waste more of our time for putting a task off. Consider how a cluttered work space physically limits our free and easy movement. We are never as productive if we are fighting for limited space. In the same way, our mental clutter, such as problems we are conscious of but have not yet solved; or negative 'baggage' we are still holding onto from our past, can hold us back from taking positive action into our future. Somehow the excuse is that such things are not the priority when there are a hundred and one more pressing jobs to complete. This diluted rating of importance is not a good thing for our peace of mind or our productivity levels. It is surprising how much psychological unrest and stress exists because we are actively trying to ignore these tasks and feelings.

We don't have to be 'big decision' procrastinators either. When we put off all the little things that we consider unimportant in the big picture, (mostly excused by having a lack of time), it eventually strips us of our ability to focus on the bigger, life changing actions. Clutter in one's mind, creates a cluttered life, period! It steals from our grasp the opportunity to be the best that we can be at anything, resulting in much less creativity, positivity and imaginative ideas.

> *"Do you know what happens when you give a procrastinator a good idea? Nothing."*
> **– Donald Gardner**

We consider cleansing our bodies on a regular basis, so why not our mind and external surroundings? There is already more than enough things in our modern world which pose as distractive forces; we don't need to add in our own unfinished business as well. So how do we overcome procrastination?

1) Recognise the detrimental impact it has on our peace of mind and effectiveness. It dictates what we get done or don't get done!

2) Make a decision to no longer procrastinate. Seize the 'bull by the horns' as they say - face the background noise that you now choose no longer to accept.

3) Spend one hour brainstorming and writing down all this background noise that is competing for attention. It maybe any number of issues such as: unfinished DIY jobs; disorganised work spaces; spring cleaning tasks; unresolved problems; 'best intentions' pushed aside and forgotten- e.g. catching up for

coffee with an old friend, or starting a project that you have kept putting off. Raise the importance of attending to these 'other' jobs. Make a list of them all. It might help to group tasks and issues together under various life areas such as: Home; Family; Work; Self.

4) Prioritise which are the most important to focus on first. Then place a timeline on the rest, so you can easily see when you ideally wish to complete and delete them...i.e. one week, one month, six months or one year.

5) Commit to taking action. The best way to attend to the tasks you have identified is to pencil them into a diary in the same way you would schedule an appointment or meeting. Allocate a certain amount of time on that day to getting the task done.

It helps to place a timeline on completion to remind you that the clock is ticking. It is the difference between doing and not doing. I remember when I was a young girl and was learning to play the electric organ... I practiced religiously every week because I knew I had to attend a weekly lesson with my instructor who would expect me to have improved my skills accordingly compared to the previous week. I didn't want to get 'found out' that I had been slack and not practiced. She kept me accountable in other words. After four years of attending lessons I decided in my 'young wisdom' that I didn't need to go anymore. I thought: "Mum and dad don't have to keep paying for lessons...I can just keep playing and further my abilities without a teacher." What do you think happened? Once I no longer had a teacher to be accountable to, I slacked off week by week and gradually hardly played at all. So in-fact I stagnated at the same level of ability that I had when I finished taking lessons.

Of course I like to defend this by saying that 'everything has it's time under the sun' and maybe organ playing had had its time! But sometimes we are not happy with ourselves for losing motivation. We might be trying to commit to a new healthy habit; or maybe we really do want to learn a new skill but keep putting it off. Sharing our intention with another person and placing a time constraint on when we intend on taking action can really help us to stay accountable and self-motivated. Once we begin to make progress deleting the backlog of jobs and addressing issues we have been guilty of ignoring, then we will start feeling the liberation that grows from completing age-old intentions. The lyrics from a well known song comes to mind:

"I can see clearly now all the rain has gone. I can see all obstacles in my way. Gone are the dark clouds that had me blind. It's gonna be a bright, bright, bright, sunshiney day."
– Jimmy Cliff

Mark Hoverson, is an empowered thought leader, speaker and highly successful online entrepreneur. He created a concept to help increase one's productivity and liberate oneself from the detrimental effects of procrastination and called it the 'Million Dollar Day'. His e-book by this same name is available on Amazon and provides a blueprint to help discharge procrastination and dissolve distractive habits. Within it he explains how to devote time and energy to recognising and then discharging what's holding us back. The book examines real accounts of people's experiences from undertaking his 'Million Dollar Day' and exposes the amazing results gained from doing it.

What I particularly found useful from learning about this practice several years ago, was recognising the detrimental impact that procrastination really can have upon us. We often underestimate how it affects our energy levels and mental state. Also, how important it is to allocate *special time* to completing all those things we continually put off. Pushing them aside does not serve us long term. Short term, yes, it appears to help free up more time in our day to day lives, but it makes us feel unsettled all the time.

Think of ourselves as a glass being filled with water each day (new information and energy). If we start each new day empty, we can eagerly await being filled with fresh, clean energising water. But if we start the day already three quarters full with old, tainted water from yesterday or perhaps even three months ago that has now become stagnant, any fresh water taken in will not stay pure and vital for long. Instead, it will become polluted by the old water in our glass and soon overflow out of our glass altogether. How much fresh, re-vitalising water are you missing out on every single day?

Chapter 14

LISTEN TO YOUR HEART, NOT JUST YOUR HEAD.

Your heart is imaginative and wise. It knows who you are, it knows what you want and it sees what you must do. To unlock your own wisdom, it is the key of kindness and compassion that will activate it every time.

When we speak of living in the heart, it does not mean we ignore our logical mind. Rather, we give ourselves permission to be actively driven by meaningful, purposeful principles, instead of relying *only* on logical reasoning. Our heart and head are as the Yin and Yang, both need the other to be a balanced whole, but when the pendulum swings too deeply into our logical mind, it causes many of us to ignore our heart's intuitive guidance. It is time that we allow the pendulum to swing right back into our heart-space, with the intention of finding equilibrium between the two.

Our logic can be very positive, offering thoughts based on self-preservation and commonsense, injecting us with logical progression and a sensible plan of action based on personal experience. Without the help of our brain's logic, we may never learn from anything that happens to us, repeating the same mistakes and making slow progress. This is the conundrum which we have to strike a balance between, for such logic can be excessively protective, it can make the false assumption that because we have failed to achieve something in the past, we will fail again in the future. The ego also resides within our logical brain and tends to be coloured by our own unique personality, with all its natural born strengths *and* weaknesses. Our ego is motivated by fear and protection of the self, so logic might sound right, but it can also be very misleading when we wish to explore places we have never been.

This is when our heart can save the day! It is always seeking to expand and explore existence more fully, enjoying variety and not minding how many times we may 'fail' before we get things right. This is because it is seeking wisdom from direct experience, rather than playing it safe and trying to make the ego 'look good'. We know that when we enter unfamiliar zone's, our logical mind can become afraid, because it does not have enough information to be guided and really only knows how to start ringing alarm bells: 'Alert! Alert! You are now entering unchartered territory...go back while you still can, I repeat, go back before it's too late!' Mmmm... what it's really saying, is go back before this new direction feels good and the positive change it will demand might break all its past assumptions and beliefs.

So how can we tell when our decisions are being governed by our head, as opposed to inspired by our heart?

- ❖ Our head is more than likely to give us a range of excuses to choose from why we should not take action.
- ❖ When we make our choices based on lack. So if our rationale is hovering only on insecurity, uncertainty, lack of ability or awareness.
- ❖ Feeling fearful is a sign of our head at work and is the 'border control' between the known and unknown, thus, it can also indicate we are avoiding a heart centred decision which may herald growth or positive change.
- ❖ When our decision is made swiftly and we are adamant it is the right one, without necessarily considering all the options available.

❖ When we refuse to take on new information before making our decision. Resistance and close mindedness is a trait of the head.

❖ Disregarding options based on judging ideas as naive, silly, unrealistic, impossible, idealistic, or impractical.

Our heart tries hard to be heard, to make it clear when we are not happy. It will come up with creative suggestions on how we could overcome issues that we don't like, without having to use escapist tactics or mental bandaids. However, without control, our logic will always step in to become the dominant influence, especially when life feels stressful and busy. Excessive 'busyness' causes us to consider ourselves time poor. When we feel time poor, we can become especially dismissive of good ideas. Our logical thought assumes a swift arrogance of knowing all the answers, closing down considerations of other alternatives. It thinks 'Less choice more certainty.' But when it narrows our outlook, it also conceals ideas that could increase our potential to be happier. *The solution is always to pause in any moment of overwhelm, breath in and ask a question instead of presume an answer.* As we learn to genuinely ask, our mind becomes more receptive to lateral, heartfelt ideas because it begins to accept that it may not have all the answers. For instance, by honestly asking the question: 'What would need to change right now for me to feel happier?' BAM! You plug straight into your heart, the process of self-reflection begins and new inspiration will start flowing into your world.

Our mind has to consciously open up to our heart and ask for its input before logic will 'step aside' for the heart to be heard. It helps to ask open, emotive questions of ourselves, those that require us to think about how we feel, rather than just seek a yes or no answer. Our logic might try to reign in such questions with very quick defined answers, but this brevity should be a warning signal that the answer is just a logical cover-up. Our heart is 'feelings' based, which means it is exploratory, expansive and experimental. If we have been closed to listening to the guidance of our heart for some time, then we will not be entirely confident in the messages it gives us for a while, but with time we will come to understand the feelings it shares as we retune to its frequency.

We all deserve hope for something better, but unless we plug into our heart before our logic, our future will always have limits. We owe it to ourselves to identify what it is that we seek and fit that pursuit in and around our responsibilities with equal priority. Unhappiness will eventually bring even the most success driven person unstuck, for we all have the need to relate ethically and meaningfully to what we do and why we do it.

Personal reflection time should be seen as showing kindness to ourselves. Interestingly, when we 'soldier on' through our ups and downs without much consideration of our own emotional wellbeing, resentment grows, towards ourselves and life in general. We begin to expect and tolerate less enjoyment from each day and even start believing that we don't *deserve* a better existence. Is this really being compassionate to us? No. We can't improve anything for the better from this state, nor will it enhance our capacity to be kind towards other people either. In fact, the bigger the chip we have sitting on our own shoulder, the less we will empathise with the difficulties that others are facing because envy and resentment can easily overshadow feelings of compassion. Envy comes when we are caught in a cycle of focusing on that which we believe we lack, rather than *what we do have to be grateful for.* By focusing only on that which we do not have, we then of course notice how much it appears in other's lives and we feel ripped off that they have what we want! The way to balance our thoughts and swing that pendulum back into our heart space, is to replace them with feelings of *abundance and gratitude.* This elevates thoughts beyond negative, selfish emotions and reminds us that we are rich beyond measure.

Indeed recognising the importance of showing kindness and

consideration to ourselves is an important progression to becoming more aligned with our heart. However, a natural flow on effect from this is to recognise opportunities to show compassion towards other people and other's needs. There are many different ways we are able to express kindness, but I'd like to explore those times when such an act is not expected, nor required of us- it is completely *our choice*. Each of us have personal triggers which spark off feelings of empathy and compassion. It might be a stranger's plight as they attempt to raise funds for their cancer treatment. Maybe homelessness is an issue we strongly resonate with, so allow those feelings to inspire us to volunteer in a local soup kitchen. Malala Yousafzai followed her heart in speaking out as a voice for women's rights, but we each connect with different ethical issues- maybe environmental protection or mistreatment of animals is more inspiring to you.

Our individual values and heart driven feelings help guide our kindness in motion. We might decide to contribute financially to a cause, but if we have more time than money, then taking direct action to assist heal the problem will be a better option. The simplest actions can often reap the most direct results. In our modern busy world, slowing down long enough to acknowledge another human being with a warm smile, hug or to listen to their worries may truly make their day. No matter what act of kindness we choose to express, our compassion slowly changes the world to be more loving and positive. Such compassionate feelings should be considered natural, healthy and freely shared to one and all.

Feeling 'moved' regularly by *something* or indeed *many things* that are happening in the world around us, is a beautiful expression that we do care about more than just ourselves. It shows that we are prepared to put our thoughts of caring generosity into action. But also, the fact we can step outside our own circumstance, recognising when *someone* is worse off than us, or *something* could be made better by directing some of our attention to it, means we have developed *heart centred perspective.* This serves us well to help lift us out of personal doldrums and re-direct our focus in a more beneficial way.

There is a Universal Law called the Law of Circulation and it refers to the movement of energy, the currency of such being traded in the form of our time, injection of positive thought, or our money. This movement of energy is sparked from various acts of contribution such as: working in an occupation to enable earning a living; caring and loving our family and friends; showing interest in community/causes; performing acts of kindness and extending friendly gestures which express compassion and consideration. Contribution is a most powerful way to transform our own life and can take many forms, but at it's core is an ability to feel kindly and compassionate. Providing our time, thought or finances is ensuring the Law provides... 'What goes around comes around.' The more freely we give, the more likely we are to receive back in a multitude of ways, not necessarily in the same way, but in a way we most need at the time. If we are loathe to contribute or participate, we will soon experience lack in our own life due to such withdrawal. Our ego sometimes creates a barrier from *allowing* us to feel appreciative of other people's generosity towards us too. If we do have trouble receiving a gesture of goodwill- even a complement- try to resolve this by accepting whatever is given with a big appreciative *thankyou* and trust that we are able to return the favour in kind, either to them or someone else, over time.

Remember, that giving does not have to be focused upon giving something which is monetarily of high value. It can simply be of value to the person receiving it. A homeless person may love and appreciate being given a hot cup of tea on a cold day; or an elderly person who lives alone with no close family, might feel on cloud nine after a ten minute conversation and receiving a sincere, warm hug. There are actually so many diverse ways of giving back. We could choose to take from one bad personal experience, the lesson which can then be shared with others, to help them overcome similar challenges. Or perhaps by becoming more self-aware and positive, we can inspire others through our happy and positive disposition?

Consistent acts of kindness, are one of the loveliest forms of giving, as they come mostly as an unexpected surprise to the recipient and not only help make someone else's day seem brighter, but it has been proven that they contribute to our own wellbeing, immunity and happy feelings, as well as to those that observe the kind act! Dr David Hamilton explores the positive side effects of kindness in his book *'The Five Side Effects of Kindness'*. One of these side effects is said to be a protective agent against cardiovascular disorders, such as high blood pressure. He explains that when we participate in random acts of kindness, this is accompanied by emotional warmth which leads to the release of oxytocins in the brain and throughout our body. Oxytocin releases a chemical called nitric oxide in blood vessels which helps to dilate them and assists to lower blood pressure. Michael J. Chase, author of *'am I being kind'* and founder of The Kindness Center in Maine, USA, also affirms the benefits of 'being kind' are indeed far reaching. In his book, he mentions that those people who practice kindness, are much more likely to experience such things as more vibrant health, confidence and self-appreciation, a deep sense of purpose and belonging, less stress, better sleep, less drama and conflict, inner peace and longer life expectancy.

I believe that apathy is the enemy of kindness, compassion and therefore happiness also. If we are never 'moved' to action in words or deeds, then nothing is touching our heart for long enough to have influence over our emotions. Thus, spreading information and taking passionate action to show our support for compassionate, respectful outcomes- be that for individuals, groups of people, our earth and any of its inhabitants, can also be considered acts of kindness by simply showing that we care about what happens to them. We can start with those who are close to us by ensuring they know how much we care for and appreciate them in our lives, rather than taking them for granted. Many are the ways we can have influence and contribute positively to help others feel good about themselves. The beautiful part about this is, when a person feels content, happy and loved, they in turn are more likely to be kinder, more generous, compassionate and understanding of others! It is a revolving cycle but it starts with one person to get the cycle turning.

Drunvalo Melchizedek writes in his book 'Living in the Heart', that our heart is actually the centre of our awareness, not our mind. He talks of long ago, when we humans were quite different and could communicate in ways that only a few in today's modern world would even begin to comprehend. A form of communication and sensing that did not involve the brain whatsoever, but rather was shared from a sacred space within the heart. This form of communicating did not involve words as such, but was more a spiritual language conveyed by feeling and trusting in our inner knowing.

He writes: 'There has always been this paradox: when a baby is conceived, the human heart begins to beat before the brain is formed. This has led doctors to wonder where the intelligence to begin and regulate the heartbeat is coming from. To the surprise of the medical world, scientists at HeartMath have discovered that the heart has its own brain- yes, a real brain with actual brain cells.'

However Drunvalo goes onto say, that an even more significant discovery by the scientists at the Institute of HeartMath in Boulder Creek, California (which is aligned with Stanford University); is perhaps that they have been able to prove that the heart generates the largest and most powerful energy field of any organ in the human body and this includes even our brain! Throughout the world's ancient writings and oral traditions, there have been references to the spiritual intelligence that resides within our sacred space of the heart, a space where we are able to co-create life and know no separation between ourselves and all other life forms.

Opening up to the possibility, that our heart potentially has far greater influence upon our thought process than our mind's logical governance, may seem unrealistic, but it has merit. *Emotive* feelings are central to our motivations and any transformational change we undertake. Our energy to see through any course of action, must be derived from that which we ethically resonate with, otherwise we always run out of steam before reaching the finish line. Our heart is a driving force to be reckoned with...but we must learn to take its guidance more seriously, so its opinions are acted upon, rather than thought of as fanciful ideology.

Our heart supports and encourages us to design bridges to reach our dreams and live the best version of our life. It also helps us recognise and be drawn to others who are also naturally heart driven. We now know, that when we are exposed to people who have bad attitudes, we too have a choice... we can allow them to influence our own feelings, dragging us into a state of negativity, or we can use them as an opportunity to strengthen our inner convictions and self-reliancy. We can't expect to be wrapped up in protective cotton wool 24/7, so rising to such challenges are an essential part of becoming a heart driven warrior!

INSPIRATION:

"Being mentally stimulated to do or feel something and be creative. A sudden brilliant or timely idea."

Chapter 15

MINDFULNESS, SELF-REFLECTION AND GRATITUDE.

These three absolutely elevate our world. Although I have talked about them to some degree previously, they really deserve their own special mention. They say the happiest people are those who have the ability to expand time and remain longer in the moment. They are reported as being able to feel a greater sense of peace, calm and positive expectation, as they are absorbing more from every second and thus giving themselves a far richer experience. Lingering for longer, gives one a chance to use our physical senses, as opposed to taking them for granted, encouraging one to really immerse into the sensation rather than experience a fleeting awareness. We are really talking about *seeing* the beauty around us and *elevating our levels of curiosity* for the how and why things have come to be. Couple this with heartfelt gratitude for simple pleasures and we begin to experience a deep seated appreciation for this gift we call 'life'.

Being busy is the greatest enemy of mindfulness. It is also our biggest excuse for why we do not live with more acknowledgment of the smaller details going on around us, but it doesn't have to be this way. We can be active observers, noticing background information even amidst our focus on daily business. In essence, this becomes an ability to *respond to and immerse in the moment at will,* despite any current task we maybe pre-occupied with. I am not referring to day dreaming or unproductive distraction, but rather the cultivation of a broader field of vision which is imprinted by more than just our own agenda for the day. It does not serve our productivity or our happiness, to become so swept up in what we are doing that we miss all the wondrous, beautiful things going on around us every day. These 'incidental' experiences can become the most powerful triggers of feelings of humility, compassion and pure amazement- which when sparked, provides us with a deep sense of profound connection and heartfelt presence to the world around us. Let's face it, in the course of achieving our agenda for the day, we can easily lose the magic- we stop seeing the forest for the trees. Have you ever scoffed down a sandwich and hardly remembered eating it, let alone appreciate the complexity of flavours and textures it provided you with? That was a missed opportunity to be in the moment. We sometimes feel that productivity gets compromised the more observant we become to smaller things going on around us. The reality however, is that short moments in appreciative observation gives us much needed respite and renewal to push effectively through our daily grind.

Self-reflection is equally important and it is also a practice which many might say they haven't any time for. But in reality, life is too short *not* to reflect on how we can or should, improve things for the better. We can often integrate such practice with times that we are more physically occupied than mentally. There are lots of occasions that we are on 'auto-pilot' and our head is free to reflect...washing the dishes is one example; driving to work is another if you live in quieter country areas and don't have to deal with city peak hour; digging over the garden; mowing the lawns; sitting on the train commuting... the list is endless really. Daily chores can sometime seem like a big time sponge, but it is possible to make them doubly productive when we selectively choose what we think about.

Self-reflection is not just about problem recognition. It can be equally about acknowledging our needs and identifying what our dreams for the future may be. It can be a time for checking in with ourselves to see how we are travelling. Personal curiosity is powerful, but we should focus on positive self-reflection, not negative churning! Reflection time is an opportunity to rise above anything going on and observe the truth. We don't have to instantly fix anything and should not let our reflection bring us down. It's more like being an objective observer on the outside looking in, whereby our intention is to be honest about our current reality. Reflection can provide essential insights into what parts of our life are coming together beautifully, whilst also allowing us to sense where it needs work before problems escalate. Notice how our emotions may change as we consider different areas. These feelings will reflect what's working and what is not. If we start to feel uptight, then look for the source of that stress; if we feel satisfied, consider we must be doing something right. Positive reflection time also has the power to filter out busy, distracted thoughts and instead allow a window of opportunity for inspired ideas to surface.

Mindfulness, self-reflection and gratitude are a powerful trio. These three help us to come to understand ourselves better, as well as our world around us. They provide the conduit to *be* in the moment, receive inspired insight and live with awareness of that which we appreciate and are grateful for. Without them, it is as though we have blinkers on, which come in the form of: distractions, denial, judgement, excessive stress, negativity and taking life for granted. This restrains our ability to see new possibilities. When we cast off these blinkers, our vision becomes expansive and yet still attuned to the finest detail. We unlock inspiration that has the potential to become our reality. Our perspective changes and we can see all that happens in a much clearer context. Complacency gets substituted by gratitude and when opportunity comes a knocking, we attune to it rather than ignoring such chance offerings.

These offerings can often come cloaked as simple synchronicities that are easily missed if we are not open to seeing them. Synchronicity aligns perfectly with both mindfulness and gratitude, as to feel its benefits, we first have to open up our heart into a state of receptivity which notices the small things going on all around us. Synchronicity refers to the nature of a thing, person, event or opportunity coming into our space of awareness, seemingly just at the right time. But it is so easy to miss such opportunities if we dismiss synchronistic occurrences as just hocus pocus! When we wallow in our own miserable emotions we miss them too. Guess what's the most effective cure-all for wallowing? Expressing gratitude. It ensures we not only appreciate what has come to us already, but enables us to expect the best of every experience.

Many call synchronicity just coincidence, but the Universe is always looking for ways to help support us and provide new insights and inspiration. Maybe just the right book comes into our field of vision at the library, or a friend gives us an audio CD to listen to, just when we needed an injection of new insight. Or perhaps we literally have someone 'stumble' into our life from opening our car door right in front of that poor pedestrian we failed to see- turns out to be the person we marry! Maybe we feel disappointed in missing out on that job we had applied for, (but were not exactly excited at the thought of getting it), only to see our dream job advertised two weeks later! Life has quite a sense of humour really, so understanding that synchronicity hovers around us at all times, can help us to look for greater meaning behind everything that transpires and puts us in a state of 'readiness' to take action when presented with such choices and opportunity.

Gratitude can be a prelude emotion to the state of mindfulness. Then consider that becoming more mindful in each moment will allow us the time to notice those little things which spark feelings of gratitude. It doesn't matter which comes first anyway, so long as we can understand that both of these states bring more vibrant experiences into our field of vision. They rest in that zone when we say 'the greatest pleasures in life cost nothing' and it is so true. But the message behind this expression is somewhat more complex *and valuable* than how it first appears, because the reality is that money *can* enable us to enjoy certain expensive activities which happen to be loads of fun! I think the intention in this saying rather, is we must first *notice* something in order for it to bring pleasure *to us*. So it reminds us that anything- even the most expensive car, sport, holiday- can be reduced to being worthless if the person experiencing it no longer appreciates key features about them. Therefore, those who master living in a state of gratitude can discover equal pleasure from a joy ride in a luxurious Maserati, as they do from taking a coastal cliff-top walk and feeling breathless from the pure raw beauty of nature.

So when we find ourselves at times feeling frustrated, with an increased desire for material 'things', 'toys', 'experiences'; try deepening our awareness for what is currently around us that we can feel incredibly grateful for. Spend time daily (often the end of the day is the best time), where we immerse in feelings of gratitude about things that have happened in our day. As we cast our mind back, we may become aware of events and observations that leave us feeling happy, proud, moved, compassionate, excited, loved, heartfelt, emotional or appreciative- all of which deepen the level at which we experience living. Instead of *skimming* over everything that goes on, we will start to feel immersed in our experiences: seeing more, sensing more, hearing more and growing far more, not from just the big events, but also from the incidental, near missed moments! This will help to increase our feelings of peace, tolerance, happiness and thankfulness.

Good ol' peace and quiet.

An important enabler of developing mindful habits, is enjoying the simplicity of peace and quiet. Surrendering to some quiet solitude on a regular basis helps us to open up more easily, become an astute observer and develop higher levels of mental clarity. It is also a powerful catalyst for firing up inspired ideas.

Spending time BY yourself provides a safe and
reassuring space for you to BE yourself.

In the presence of others, we are often more self conscious and that can result in effecting even the thoughts we allow ourselves to think. This is particularly true if we tend to be a person who tries hard to please others. Inspiration is more likely to flow when we seek out regular alone time, as we begin to re-program our mind to let down its guard against the influence or control of significant others around us. Only once such filters of influence are removed, is it likely that our mind will plug into our own personal source of inspired possibility.

When I speak of quiet solitude, I do not mean simply being by ourselves. I also mean switching off all forms of distraction that will prevent or interrupt streams of reflection time, such as mobile phones, computers, television and radio. Nor am I talking of spending some down time just reading a good book! I refer to creating regular times where we *tune out* from our everyday life, to-do lists and worries. It is time to contemplate what we may not normally allow ourselves time to ponder. Our intention should be, to empty our mind of most thoughts, responding instead to the moment going on around us. This helps to tune into our natural surroundings and sense who we are in the scheme of things. We abruptly pause our attention slavery towards 'background noise' and free up room for other thoughts to pop into our mind that we don't give the time to otherwise. To begin with, switching off like this can seem difficult.

Meditation can be one form of quieting the mind, but we do not have to formally meditate. This is where simple mindfulness can help traverse the void. Turning our attention to what is going on around us, whether we are out walking in nature; sitting in quiet observation in our backyard; taking a relaxing bath; or even stroking our dog; the intention should be to allow the space to drift fully into the present moment at hand. We can gently re-direct thoughts from the past or future to thinking about the now instead, becoming more conscious of how we feel and what we are sensing...

Inhale the aromas aloft on the air; feel the breeze tickling your hair; sense textures against your skin; really see the scenery around you; tune into every noise you can detect close to you and in the distance. Quiet contemplation about everything happening right now... not yesterday, not last year, not tomorrow or a month from now. Simply reflect on all that is within your range of sensory detection, right NOW.

Relaxing music is an exception to 'background noise' as it can be considered to be a positive catalyst to inspire and slow down our intrusive thoughts during desired quiet solitude. It is especially useful when we wish to slow down our mind, but we maybe in a noisy, man-made environment. By putting on ambient music, it helps to screen out the other distracting sounds by giving us something else to focus and even immerse our attention upon. Some people enjoy a similar experience of drawing themselves into the moment, by playing a tranquil musical instrument such as a Tibetan singing bowl, hank drum or even piano.

Quiet, contemplative times allow us the space to ponder, appreciate and dive right into the moment...and that is when inspired ideas can magically begin to flow. Childlike curiosity and fascination is part of our nature if we just give ourselves the time and freedom to still feel it. Take away all the 'white noise' and we begin to tune into the guidance of our own heart.

Chapter 16

IGNITE YOUR INSPIRED SPARK!

To connect with our *purpose and passion* we turn up the volume on a meaningful existence. We began to explore what lights our fire a little in Chapter 12. The quiz you completed will have served to identify what matters most to you, from your most ethical and value driven core. There is however, more to this subject of inspiration, than just finding your passion and purpose. Inspiration comes from different sources serving different needs; but essentially, the more *open-minded* you become, the greater chances of inspired thought flowing into your mind and world.

Who or what is an inspired person?

'The inspired person looks for any opportunity to shine a glimmer of light and joy upon even the most mundane task. They recognise their heart as a guiding light and even when their head get's in the way, their heart will be a persistent beacon, always reminding them of what's most important. The inspired person knows that when something goes adrift, there will be a reason for it and will look for any sign of synchronicities or a lesson to be learnt from the experience. Their mind is open, imagining new realities beyond the borders of conformity. New information is used to help change perspective if they feel their life has switched onto go-slow with nothing quite 'working'. They consider a change in direction, or any change period, is not to be feared, but seen as a catalyst to grow new inspired possibility. All of these traits pave the way towards experiencing and being fully conscious

of inspired thought when it hits. Such an individual will throw more fuel on a new idea, rather than dismiss and extinguish a pilot flame.'

The difference between an inspired person and one who is simply logical, is they feel no restraint in considering options available to them. They are living in life's flow, where new ideas are floating by in an abundant river of dreams. All that they must do is reach out and take hold of just one of these ideas, faithfully believing in their capacity to bring it forth to fruition.

Our self-belief is paramount. We also know that it is the thoughts we keep that provide the fertile soil to incubate ideas and successfully turn them into actions. Often we take no action at all because the minute we have an idea, we begin worrying about the *how* rather than believe in our *why*. On auto-pilot we often ask the wrong question first: 'But how on earth could I ever make that happen?' Just *stop* that thought process and substitute a more curious question... 'Who would that serve best and why would that make me feel good?' Instantly we tap into awareness of our *why* and whether the idea has merit to anchor our focus.

Faith is the next important step. Know in our heart that if there exists the right *why*, the journey is already laid out before us. We may not yet know every step, but it will gradually unfold in a timeline which is just as it should be. Sometimes we obsess over getting quickly to the destination but it is secretly the journey we need the most anyway, so let it just reveal itself and try to release control over the outcome. *Everything* that happens to us or through us, provides us with further learning and experience and *that* is what is most important.

Inspiration can potentially flow in all facets of our existence, but it particularly flows more naturally when we seek to experience happiness, not just practical/material benefit from our chosen activities. We all deserve to feel a deep profound joy from what we do, not just tick something off our 'to-do list'. But this takes thought and consideration on our part and sometimes we don't slow down long enough to discover how best we should meet our needs. I'll give you an example of this, in the life area of fitness and exercise. Why go to the gym for a workout if all it seems to us is a chore? We can achieve fitness goals by doing this, but is it going to elevate our mood naturally because we actually feel happy doing it? Sure physical movement does come with the side benefit of releasing feel-good endorphins, but why not capitalise on this and create a double whammy effect? We can do this by actively designing the type of exercise routine which will not just work our body, but feel fun whilst we are working out! This will result in us sticking with our new habit *and* looking forward to doing it.

Personally, I find the *what* and *where* I do exercise does matter. I enjoy going walking and I prefer it to be a peaceful environment where I am surrounded by nature. This has the added benefit of relaxing my mind and releasing tension, because for me, nature provides solace and elevates my mood. For someone else their preference maybe jogging around an athletics track as it provides a more structured, formal training environment which makes it easier to calculate the exact distance run and remain focused on an intense workout. I also love dance as exercise, but the music I *choose to dance to* is paramount to me enjoying the act of dancing. It would not necessarily work as well if I went to classes and followed steps to a dance instructor's own choice in music as I naturally prefer spontaneous movement to whichever music takes my fancy at the time. My point is this...we are all born perfectly unique for a reason. We have the power of choice to remain loyal to our own inner voice and participate in activities which express that individuality. Society however, mostly tries to convince us of the opposite, that it is preferable to behave like others and desire similar things. But you are you and your choices must reflect that authentically, otherwise you will never get excited by any type of routine you set in place.

So I encourage you to become very involved in designing your life, in your own unique way, beginning with the mundane activities right through to crafting your vision for the future. Challenge yourself to try making that repetitious task more tolerable and even fun. We are never too old to be playful in our approach to anything! For instance, let's use housework as an example: I turn the music on extra loud as I vacuum the floors (it makes me feel good *and* no-one can hear me singing either!) I'm sure there are plenty of you out there who choose to do housework to music? I have heard of some people who find that changing into a different set of clothes (like a uniform), may get them 'in the mood' to complete certain jobs they don't like and it also works well for doing exercise. I also consider life's too short to always rush to get stuff done...we deserve to take a bit of extra time to talk to one another, joke about, take a break, have a cuppa and breathe. If we at first begin by trying to invigorate the smaller mundane chores we do, then gradually we seek to find happiness in every facet of our life, goals and dreams.

In other words, we *raise the bar.* Small habits always lead to bigger beliefs. It is good to have high expectations to genuinely feel fulfilled from all the little moments we put together and collectively label it *our life.* Dramas and derailments are only temporary when we hold strongly to a positive default belief of being deserving of and naturally expecting our experiences to be genuinely good and progressively improve. Allowing ourselves to be guided by such positive expectation will always raise our spirits, encourage our creativity and ensure that pilot flame of inspired thought never fades.

When inspiration flows, how do you judge if an idea is good, bad or indifferent?

Ideas can completely change the direction we take into the future. That is why it is helpful to ask ourselves a few questions to decipher the merit of an idea and to establish if it is really worth exploring further.

The first question to ask is: Does it align with my ethics and values?

The second: Does it serve or bring positive benefit to others as well as myself?

The third: Will it demand more of me...will I need to grow as a result of bringing it to fruition?

The fourth: Does the idea of it excite me and make me feel more alive?

Pursuing anything which enhances our own growth and self-awareness is a good thing, because with greater introspection we also develop greater empathy towards other people. Our values dictate that we must act in accordance with them, otherwise we will lose motivation. A similar loss of steam will result if our pursuit is only self-serving, as we are all naturally encouraged when our actions also have a positive effect on others. This benefit might turn out to be direct or indirect. An example of a *direct benefit* could be setting up a charity raising funds for a specific worthy cause. An *indirect benefit* might be encouraging our children to follow their own dreams, by walking our talk and living authentically. If our idea excites us, then we will become more energised, vibrant and fun to be around- that's a no brainer and speaks for itself!

Finding inspiration through trial and error is sometimes the best way!

We mustn't get despondent when we find ourselves in the midst of a chaotic period of trying new things but making mistakes and feeling confused. Experimentation and exploration is part of an adventure which helps us to increasingly make better choices. Deepak Chopra likes to put it like this:

"All great changes are preceded by chaos."

Let's face it, often the closer we come to the changes we need most, we are becoming more and more honest with ourselves about what currently is not working and causing us distress. This can create a whole range of emotions and overwhelm us with the thought of the task ahead. The light bulb moment we might have expected to have could still be eluding us and we find ourselves a little lost in trying to move forward with conviction. Sounds a bit of a disaster doesn't it? I call it the *phase of uncertainty* and it is completely natural. It calls upon us to have faith in the process and allow ourselves a period of trial and error. None of us can ever be certain of the right course of action, but so long as we hold to an open mind, be willing to seek new information to support/direct our journey and actively try different methods to solve our problems, then we will be on *the right journey*.

I think it is good to realise that when we feel in a state of flux and rather unsure about the next step, this can provide the spark we need to ignite a new fire beneath us. Look to safety in our own self-belief, so we do not have to rely on another person to support every step we take, as they simply may not understand what is going on for us. Trust that we are growing as we experiment. It may leave us feeling a little exposed, but we will be learning and expanding at the same time.

> *"Faith is a bird that feels dawn breaking*
> *and sings while it is still dark."*
> **– Rabindranath Tagore.**

Remember that self-belief is about building faith and trust in our own gut feelings and heartfelt intuition. Certainty is always an illusion, so the fact we may lack assuredness of any particular outcome should not prevent us starting to make change. Have faith to find our own unique path and accept that we will see the occasional 'wrong way go back' signs telling us to try another approach. Courage, rather than perfectionism will always serve us much better. Such is the territory of self-discovery...it's an exciting road to tread.

Chapter 17

ENTER FREEDOM AND LIVE HAPPINESS.

Conscious living is the key that unlocks the door to our mind and allows freedom to enter. Being conscious means living with awareness, of our own self and the impact we have on others. It is the ability to reflect upon what's been and gone, so that we can act more positively in the here and now. To be conscious means to be flexible and yet also actively directive of the course we take rather than feeling pushed here and pulled there by some unknown force. Complacency does not have a place to take hold when one lives with conscious awareness.

Freedom resides within our heart. When we tune our heart's frequency, it helps us to cast aside the fears that prevent us examining who we are and getting to know what the future *could* hold. When we question the meaning behind our existence, there is one thing which is and has always been truth. I have said it before, but it's worth saying again: *Our Life* is a miracle and *we* are a miracle, so the meaning we attach to our experience of living here on Earth should be equally as expansive without limits. Hold onto this magical perspective, for when we lose touch with it, complacency tries to settle in and rob us of happiness. *Nothing* should be considered ho hum, mediocre or lacking; this view is just a momentary blindness missing the amazing complexity of reality.

Never be afraid to look at the world from a different angle, even if it's not the opinion of the majority. To live in expectation of a higher level existence will dictate the direction we move. The liberation of personal freedom takes hold once we *claim our ability to create an extraordinary experience* from wherever we find ourselves sitting right now. Our readiness for expansion into the very best version of us, is the way we thank the Universe for our Life.

Self-defeating habits can be overcome by our own choice to do so. The human mind has the ability to become increasingly more responsive than reactive. We can adopt new habits through fostering daily rituals and provide ourselves with powerful motivation using reminders of benefits expected from action taken. If we approach our failures as being equally life transforming as our successes, this will build optimism and courage, helping us to overcome inbuilt fears that limit our progress.

When someone is stagnating and not changing at all, it tends to be done with no awareness of it, or certainly none that is admitted. It often will take a big shake up in their world to shock them into the state of conscious awareness again. These types of experiences are often not only life-changing, but actually life-saving. Personal freedom ends when we stagnate by keeping everything certain and the same. The analogy has always been if we are not growing, we are dying. Well, I consider it is more a case of remaining stunted until our last breath, which is probably much worse, as we remain in a state of repeated suffering.

Many years ago I bought a decorated block to sit on the mantel piece as a present for my partner and for all in our family to be reminded of the words it had inscribed upon it:

> *"Life is not measured by the breaths you take, but the moments that take your breath away."*

I do not believe such moments have to be unbelievably sensational. These moments however, must be noticed to be entirely enjoyed. Ordinary, everyday occurrences can be made exceptionally special and yes even breathtaking, just by directing our full attention towards them and discarding idle distractions. Allowing ourselves to be distracted by things of little importance in the big picture, robs our lives of discovering real meaning and becoming fully conscious of that which deserves to be acknowledged.

Expanding into our own 'free self' will take courage and experimentation, but any journey must always begin with taking that first step to move beyond what we have always done or known. Growth is the right arm man of freedom and the more we experiment with getting to know who we are and what our purpose maybe, the greater our potential for growth and new insights of self awareness. Material certainty is not what brings us happiness. It is the knowledge that we are living authentically, bravely walking our talk in full trust of our inner voice, rather than pretending we can't hear it over all the excuses we hold onto. The disempowered voice within us, or from someone else, will never cease to argue the point over the choices we make and the direction our journey takes, but nor will our heartfelt intuition be silent. Just as we have the ability to choose which radio station we tune into, so too can we make a decision as to which voice we will attune to and allow to live stream!

Trust that when inspiration comes upon us it most likely will ask more of us. Our heart always wants us to become more rather than less. We have spoken about how our challenges often force us through experiences that are not always pleasant, but we still have the choice to use some of that unpleasantness for good! Own your experiences and what they have gifted you in the process...such things as knowledge of real achievements; bravery in tolerating hard times; and the ability to love despite the hardships you've endured. Let this awareness expand your vision for what is possible in the future. Allow every experience to touch your perspective as another lesson colouring who you are. Expand your vision of what this life means to you. We don't need to stay any particular course just because it is safer, what's expected of us, or what we thought was right yesterday. Our freedom evolves as we allow our direction to shift in response to not what we have known, but what we are learning right now.

Snowflake Imaginings...

"Imagine yourself to be a little snow flake that decided to take a risky chance one day, by falling from the sky onto a very steep slope, high above the gully where most of the other snowflakes decide to fall. You had such a sensational view from way up there- you were able to see the world from a completely different perspective to most others. You could see beyond your own self and see glimpses of the entire landscape in all its miraculous beauty, enabling you to understand there was so much more to this world than what first meets the eye. But then the earth starts to shake and suddenly you find yourself hurtling down the mountain, you have been swept up inside an enormous thundering avalanche. The more you roll, the quicker you gather size and momentum- you feel as though you have no choice but to take the most direct, shortest route and not deviate. Then as suddenly as it began, you come to an abrupt, explosive halt as you smash against a large rocky outcrop and rain down as an individual flake upon the valley floor below. There you land upon the head of a creature you have never seen- it's a panda bear who seems absolutely oblivious to the tumultuous adventure you were just a part of. You sit there exhausted. You feel disconnected from who you were at the top of the mountain, so much has just happened. Never have you experienced such a rush of emotions and movement. Now you have a completely different view from where you sit. You lament the loss of your expansive view from high up the mountain but see that you were one of the lucky ones to land up there in the first place. Some flakes never got to experience first-hand that perspective in their lifetime. You recall how it felt fleetingly to be more expanded and powerful as a snowball racing down the mountainside and yet to be mobilised as a single flake on this panda's head exploring the valley floor feels no less incredible. You suddenly feel astounded at your awakening, happy in the moment and excited for what tomorrow will bring."

Our view can change in a heartbeat, but it is our perspective and emotion we hold about that which befalls us that dictates in this moment what our experience will be. Happiness is tied to our interpretation of whether we consider what happens is good, but what if it *just is*? We are living a sequence of present moments that are being created continually in the now and this gives us the power to influence what happens next and choose how it affects us. The minute we believe nothing can change, is the moment that life appears to have no meaning...happiness will become just a distant memory.

Pursue the dreams you hold close to your heart. Waiting until all elements come into perfect alignment is *not* the answer as you know that moment will never come: there is always risk; you will never be certain of the outcome; self-confidence is never unshakeable; responsibilities will always be pressing. Waiting only allows an endless spectrum of excuses to stand between you and your inspired ideas.

There is an ancient Chinese proverb which says:

> *"The best time to plant a tree was twenty years ago, the second best time is now."*

This lifetime will not last forever. It is special and deserves your full attention. Let yourself feel the inner urgency of what is really important to create your most meaningful experience and go after it as though there is no tomorrow! Your happiest and most extraordinary life is waiting in the wings for you to just make it centre stage...

THE END

About the Author

A certified Life Coach and Holistic Counsellor,
Lynda Ford lives with her family in the
beautiful Southern Australian bush.
She believes it is important in this fast paced material
world to reclaim one's connection with nature and heart
based wisdom in the face of intellectual dominance.
Her career has reflected a love and curiosity for
people and nature, encompassing Permaculture,
Natural Therapies and Community Services.
You can connect with more of her thoughts
and guidance at: www.wildbanksia.com

Printed in the United States
By Bookmasters